THE HAMMER AND THE FROG,

GOD WATCHES OUT FOR ME

THE HAMMER AND THE FROG,
GOD WATCHES OUT FOR ME

Floyd E. Friedli

WestBow
PRESS
A DIVISION OF THOMAS NELSON

WestBow Press books may be ordered through booksellers or by contacting:

WestBow Press
A Division of Thomas Nelson
1663 Liberty Drive
Bloomington, IN 47403
www.westbowpress.com
1-(866) 928-1240

Because of the dynamic nature of the Internet, any web addresses or links contained in this book may have changed since publication and may no longer be valid. The views expressed in this work are solely those of the author and do not necessarily reflect the views of the publisher, and the publisher hereby disclaims any responsibility for them.

Certain stock imagery © Thinkstock.
Any people depicted in stock imagery provided by Thinkstock are models, and such images are being used for illustrative purposes only.

ISBN: 978-1-4497-2680-5 (e)
ISBN: 978-1-4497-2681-2 (sc)
ISBN: 978-1-4497-2682-9 (hc)

Library of Congress Control Number: 2011916447

Printed in the United States of America

WestBow Press rev. date: 9/23/2011

Contents

I dedicate this book to my wife, Patricia, our son, Evan, and my parents, who gave me the fantastic life experiences that have made this book possible. The editing by Lynn Frank and her suggestions were invaluable.

1. Introduction

I truly believe God is watching out for me, which is hard to fathom, as I am just an ordinary person with a number of human faults. I've always felt there was a God, and he looked after and protected me. My parents were Presbyterian and raised me as such. We went to church every Sunday, and I attended Sunday school before the service. My parents were always very active in the church, worked on committees, and donated generously. They were believers but did not seem overly religious. They taught me the fundamentals, but by about sixth grade, I felt God or a general goodness of being.

This book relates a number of my life experiences that have convinced me there is definitely a God. My life has been spared a number of times, and he has taught me a number of valuable lessons. I hope to convey my beliefs to you and let you see the goodness in life. My philosophy of life is still evolving, but I will try to let you see my thoughts and beliefs. God seems to be looking out for me for no reason I can discern, other than maybe because I believe. I hope he is looking out for you, and you can feel his presence.

Outwardly, I do not appear very religious. I could attend church more and be more active. I don't profess my beliefs to others often, because I am a private person. I certainly don't try to convert anyone to Christianity. I do enjoy a good religious or political discussion at a party or a gathering, if everyone involved is open-minded and listens to others in the discussion; however, religion and politics are so infused with emotion that few people can engage in a discussion where various beliefs and points of view are expressed. I hope this book allows you to examine your beliefs and see what makes sense to you, what feels right in your gut. My beliefs are strong, and I hope to make yours stronger.

In The Hammer and the Frog, I describe (1) important events in my life, (2) some of my philosophies, (3) how I arrived at my beliefs, and (4) my thoughts on how the world should be.

2. Hammer and the Frog—
Near-Death Experiences

I don't know what is typical during a person's life. I only know my experiences and what I have seen of my family and friends' lives. I have had a number of near-death experiences. Maybe they were not true near-death experiences, but they were as close as I want to come to ending my life. The following are events that scared me. You probably have a number of your own.

Tree-Climbing Contest

When I was a little kid, we lived on the edge of town, near creeks, small hills, and many trees. I was fairly agile at that age and would climb the trees in our neighborhood with my friends. We were like a little band of monkeys, knowing no fear of heights. In the nice weather, I would be outside, playing with my friends and running around the neighborhood. But my mother did not know what we were really doing, as she would have stopped me before I got hurt. We would routinely climb twenty to thirty feet up the various trees in our area, going out as far as the limbs would support our weight.

I was eleven in 1962, and Jay Kitchens and I were having a tree-climbing contest. The empty lot next to my parents' house had four full-grown maple trees in a row. We had never climbed those trees before, as the lower limbs were hard to reach. The trees were also too close to my mother's watchful eyes. In the contest, Jay and I had each climbed the first, third, and fourth of the trees, but neither of us could make it up the second tree. The lowest limbs were too high, and the trunk was too thick to get a good grip. As a last resort, we decided to cheat and build a rope ladder. While coming down, my feet got tangled in the ladder, and I fell head-first to the ground, twenty feet below. I put out my left arm just in time to break my fall. Well, there was a break all right, and it was my left arm. The bottom bone could be set in standard fashion, but I needed surgery to get the tendons out from between the parts of the upper bone. By all rights, I should have broken my neck and been dead or at least a quadriplegic. Why had I been spared? I truly believe God was watching out for me and, for some reason, spared my life and mobility.

What did I learn from the fall? Not much! I suppose if God were really an interventionist, he would have tripped me on the way to climb the rope ladder to give me the hint not to do this sort of thing.

Because of the fall, I slowly developed a fear of heights and do not like to get more than about ten feet above ground. If I have to put up a ladder to do some work on our house, I really start to get scared at about the one-story mark.

Frog Baseball

Kids do many incredibly stupid things, so it is lucky that most of us actually make it to adulthood. It was a hot summer day, and I was about twelve. All the neighborhood kids were out running around and playing. One of us caught a frog hopping around in the yard. Brad, who had a sadistic streak, suggested we play baseball with the frog. We couldn't find a baseball bat, but Nick found a ball-peen hammer in his garage. One kid would toss the frog underhand, like a softball, and Brad would take a swing at it with the hammer. Who would really think of a game this disgusting? I realized this was really gross and dangerous, so I backed up about fifty feet and leaned against a tree. Fortunately, the frog wiggled so much in the air that Brad could not hit it. On about the tenth swing, Brad lost control of the hammer. It flew about fifty feet, and the metal head hit me right in the jaw. Two inches lower and it would have hit me in the throat; one inch higher and I would have lost most of my teeth; four inches higher and I could have lost an eye; and six inches higher and I would have been hit in the forehead and seriously hurt or killed. Surprisingly, it hit me exactly in the middle of the jaw and only cost me a few stitches. No broken bones—nothing except looking incredibly stupid and uncoordinated for not being able to get out of the way of a flying hammer. Again, it seems like someone was watching out for me.

I-71

Pat and I were not married yet, and we were driving back to Cleveland to her parents' house. It was not a bad day, but there was some slight rain. We were about ten miles south of Cleveland on Interstate 71. About a half mile ahead, I saw a car with its brake lights on, and I assumed the driver just tapped his brakes to slow down a little. As we got closer, I realized the other car had come to a complete stop, and I was approaching him at about seventy-five miles per hour. I slammed on my brakes. We spun around several times and ended up in the left lane, facing the traffic. Fortunately, no one was near us when we spun around. No car was coming at us directly at least for about a half mile. I was able to restart the car quickly and pull off onto the median. Pat and I were really shaken up but unhurt. I asked her how she was, and she said she was fine but upset. We sat there a few minutes to collect ourselves and then, when a break in the traffic came, I pulled out and turned the car around. Several things had to occur just right; otherwise, Pat and I would have been killed or seriously injured. Was it coincidence or someone watching over us?

Almost Drowning in the Bahamas

My mother signed me up for several years of swimming lessons when I was seven, so I was always a pretty good swimmer. After about six years in our first house, my wife, Pat, and I put a swimming pool in our backyard. I was thirty-one and, thanks to swimming, was in good condition. We went on a vacation to Paradise Island in the Bahamas. At that time, we stayed at a Holiday Inn on a picturesque bay. The area has been completely redone and is now the Atlantis

Resort. At that time, the bay was about a half mile across and about twelve feet deep in the middle.

On the second day of our trip, I decided I was strong enough to swim across the bay. At just about the halfway point, I realized the swim was longer than I thought and was much more difficult in the ocean. There weren't any sizable waves in the protected bay, but it was not like a swimming pool. As I was getting tired, I looked down and noticed the bottom was about twelve feet below me. After looking back, forward, and to the side, I realized I was about the same distance from all areas of the shore. I started to panic but realized my options were limited: drown or keep swimming. I took a few deeps breaths and started to swim. I kept going and finally reached the other side. I'm normally a high-strung person in emergency situations, but I was somehow able to calm myself and get out of this mess. Later, I thought maybe God was taking care of me.

Now that I had proved I could swim across the bay, and quickly forgetting my recent harrowing experience, I swam the bay twice a day for the rest of our trip. I was really getting in great shape. That bay, now called Cove Beach at the Atlantis Resort, is still a fantastic beach for swimming or snorkeling, but because they have it roped off with buoys, you can no longer do my exact swim.

Ammonia at Mapleton

As a chemist, I spent most of my time in the corporate research and development lab in Dublin, Ohio. However, several times a year, I would travel to our Mapleton, Illinois, plant to attend project meetings, do a plant trial on a process modification we developed, or help run a new product in production. On this occasion in 1989, I had been at the plant several days to help start up a new reactor. After my lunch break, I walked back to the reactor area and noticed no one was around. This seemed very strange, and suddenly, I got a big whiff of ammonia. Diluted ammonia is useful in household cleaning and as a farm fertilizer, but concentrated ammonia will literally take your breath away, and it did mine. I couldn't breathe and could only hold what breath I had. My eyes were burning and watering. I looked around in desperation and saw all the plant workers from our building standing across the street, waving for me to come toward them. I continued to hold my breath and ran very clumsily to their location and gasped a breath of fresh air.

Apparently, an ammonia compressor had blown its seal, releasing a few pounds of liquid ammonia into the reactor building. Everyone evacuated. If I had collapsed, people might not have seen me. Even if they had, they could not have helped me without risking their lives. Only a firefighter or a rescue worker wearing a respirator could have helped me then. Another close call, but someone gave me the strength to make it out unharmed.

Fiero on Icy Bridge

It was 1988, and I was coming back from a business trip, driving home from the airport in a light but messy snowstorm. My little car (a Pontiac Fiero) was adequate in the ice and snow, but not great. I knew that I had to be careful, but I was tired and got sloppy. I wasn't thinking and gave the car some gas as I was crossing a bridge on I-270 around Columbus. I knew better than this, and I started to lose control. I ended up spinning out and doing several revolutions before coming to a stop on the berm. Had other cars or trucks been near me or behind me, I would have been in serious trouble. My little car would have been roadkill for a semi. But again, I was fine. I turned the car around and went home, thanking God for overcoming my stupidity once again. It would have been so easy to become a statistic, but it was not my time yet.

Swimming in Kauai

About three years ago, Pat and I were vacationing in Kauai with our son and his fiancée Jessica (Gigi). Kauai is known for high winds and rough surf, depending on the time of the year. I went in for my normal ocean swim, which is usually about a four-hundred-yard swim parallel to the shore in water about four feet deep. I was swimming away, watching the shore and the water depth to try to remain the same distance from the shore. I like to swim with the shore on my right, so every time I move my head to the right to take a breath, I get a view of the shore. When my head is facing down into the water, I try to check the depth. I was enjoying the swimming more than I was paying attention to my safety. I stopped swimming for a rest and was surprised I was in over my head and could not touch the bottom. Funny: this incident sounds like a previous episode of stupidity.

Apparently, my swim had angled out into the ocean, and I was not parallel to the coastline. Also, the shore dropped off quicker than I thought, making the water deeper. I started to swim toward shore and after about twenty seconds, stopped and tried to touch the bottom—without luck. After doing this three or four times, I realized I was not making any progress and must be in an undertow or an outgoing current. I started to panic and realized my wife was not going to be able to help. My son was too far down the beach to help, and there was no lifeguard. I tried to calm myself, but this didn't work very well. So, I started to swim toward shore in earnest and kept trying to touch bottom. After what seemed an eternity, but was probably only a minute or two, I got close enough to shore to barely touch bottom. I tried to walk in, but the current was very strong. So, after a combination of swimming and walking for another five minutes, I was standing on shore.

While I believe God protects me, he cannot always protect you if you refuse to use common sense. I should have known better. The surf was rough, and I should have paid attention. While this was a similar incident to what happened in the Bahamas almost thirty years ago, I'm not the swimmer I once was. I had been in real danger this time!

Changing Lanes

As I have gotten older, I don't drive as fast as I used to; now I usually go only a few miles an hour over the speed limit. About five years ago, I was cruising down I-270, which circles the city of Columbus, Ohio, running some errands around town. I got caught up in listening to my stereo and the nice ride of my car. Suddenly, I realized I was about to miss my exit. I was in the wrong lane, being on the far left and a long way from exiting on the right. Not wanting to miss my exit, I checked the next lane for traffic and then floored the gas pedal, barely getting around several cars just in time to miss a large concrete barrier and get off the exit. Once safely on the off-ramp, a shiver came over my body, as I realized the utter brainlessness of my actions and how close I came to killing myself and others. Had I not been in a good car or had the pavement been slippery, I would have missed the exit and hit the concrete barrier.

Again, God can only help you so much. There seems to be a theme in my near-death experiences—stupidity, followed by help from above to let me escape unharmed.

3. Patricia—Love of My Life

I was not given great social skills. People seem to like me but are not drawn to me. Like my father, I lack charisma; therefore, I was not very successful in the dating scene in high school or college. It took me a long time to work up the courage to ask a girl out, and then I was not very adept at actually asking her when I took that step. I had a hard time getting girls to go on dates with me, and if they did go, they would not go out too many times before deciding I was boring and not for them. I was not looking for one-night stands, but I was looking for a steady girlfriend. So, I found myself rather lonely in college. I remember being somewhat depressed one day in college and kind of asking myself and God what the matter was with me. I needed a girlfriend to take care of and love.

Sometime in the next six months, I was walking through the Music Department of the College of Wooster, when Patricia Smith was sitting on the edge of a big, wooden table in the lobby, swinging her legs back and forth. I had seen her numerous times in the music building and in concert band; she played clarinet, while I played the trumpet. Patricia had even dated my roommate, Bob, for several months, and they recently parted ways. I knew Pat, but not well.

She looked at me, smiled, and said, "You know, I don't have a date for Friday's cello concert. No one has asked me out to that." I am slow, but I can take a hint, so I said I would be glad to take her to the cello concert. You have to be really lonely to be glad to take a date to a cello concert! So, Friday night I picked her up at the college house where she was staying, and we walked to the cello concert.

Only then did I realize I had been somewhat hustled. Pat was the piano accompanist for Dick James's senior cello recital. So, I sat in the first row by myself, watching Pat play the piano to Dick's cello music. After the concert, there was a reception/party back at her house. She was unbelievably beautiful, charming, exciting, and fun to be around. She flirted all the time and made everyone like her. Pat had all the social skills I lacked.

Patricia was a very unusual person in that she would date anyone once. She did not prejudge their appearance or initial conversation skills; she would go out with them and see what they were like. Most men and women prejudge people and only date those who have some attractive qualities that show the relationship might move forward. Pat would give everyone a chance, assuming that if the date was a total bust, she had at least given them a chance and might get a dinner or a movie out of the evening. I think Pat dated almost forty guys, and I was number thirty-six. Once I had spent a few hours with her, I was hooked and definitely wanted to spend more time with her. Like most women, she was not drawn to me, but at least she was willing to see me again occasionally. We dated about six times in the next five months.

During that summer break, she came down to Coshocton, Ohio, to spend the weekend with my parents and me. A few weeks later, I want to Cleveland to spend a weekend with Pat and her parents. Carnival rides—especially roller coasters—have never been an interest of mine, and I avoided them. Pat loved roller coasters, so on my trip to Cleveland, she took me to Cedar Point amusement park in Sandusky, Ohio. Cedar Point has always been one of the premier roller-coaster parks in the country, adding new death-defying rides every year or so. Pat, of course, wanted to ride every ride in the park, and not wanting to appear to be a wimp, I gladly agreed. When we came down the first hill of the Blue Streak, I thought my heart was going to explode, and I was going to die. I had never been on a ride like this. Guys will do almost anything to impress a girl! We rode every ride in the park that day.

At one point early in the fall of my junior year, when I was getting more serious about Pat, she tried to discourage me by saying,

"I only really date guys at least six feet fall." I'm only 5'8", while Pat is 5'7". I thought, *Well, at least we have a challenge now. I'm not going to give up on her.*

The competitive suitors dropped by the wayside, one at a time. I was always there, getting a little more charming, a little smoother, a little more interesting all the time. I bought her cute little gifts and flowers, and eventually, she was hooked. By then, she was a senior in college, and I was in my first year of graduate school at Ohio State, an hour and a half away. She had gone from the girl who could somewhat tolerate me to the girl who would wiggle her ring finger and say, "There is nothing on this finger. Why is that?" Again, I'm socially slow, but I took the hint and gladly proposed to her in spring of 1974. We were married a few years later and have been happily married for over thirty-four years now.

Did God have a hand in this? I certainly believe so!

When you are just meeting someone and falling in love, you discuss ordinary topics. You talk about your daily activities or your next social event. At a later point, you may discuss religion or politics or philosophies on saving and spending money. Even later, you will discuss where you want to live, what type of house, and how you want it furnished and decorated. What is amazing to me is how compatible Pat and I are. We agree very closely on religion and politics. Since she is Catholic and from a big city and I am Presbyterian from a small town, we could have had vastly different views. We agree on almost everything—from picking out furniture to choosing a vacation, getting a pet, or buying a car.

4. Graduate School—
He Taught Me a Lesson

After graduating from the College of Wooster in chemistry, I went to The Ohio State University to get a PhD in organic chemistry. The OSU Chemistry department was one of the top-fifteen graduate programs in the country and unbelievably rigorous. It was all I could handle to pass the courses, the general qualifying exams, the cumulative exams on special topics, and complete some original, breakthrough research. But I studied hard and passed everything with decent, but not fantastic, grades.

At one stage, each candidate had to pass four "cumulative exams" on special, state-of-the-art topics. You had fifteen tries to pass four exams. The tests were almost impossible. These two-hour torture tests were administered at 9 a.m. one Saturday a month. Since it took me eleven tries to pass four, this torture went on for almost a year. Many times, fifteen minutes into the test, I would say to myself, *I have no idea what the professor is talking about, and I am going to flunk this test. Looks like I wasted a Saturday morning. I should have slept in.* The worst thing about the process was the self-doubt. If you could not pass the tests, you could not get a PhD. Every flunked test blew a hole in your ego and self-confidence. I saw a number of students, equal or better than I, leave after a few years with a master's rather than a PhD or with no advanced degree, because they could not handle the pressure or last through the entire process.

The pass-fail list for the cumulative exams was posted about a week after the test, so you went down to the basement and looked at the list and either jumped for joy or dropped your head in shame and slinked out of the building. I did more slinking than jumping. Twice, I was the "high flunk," having achieved the highest score that was just below the arbitrary cut line. Even my own professor made me the high flunk on one test. Some politics were involved, because most professors seemed to draw the cut line just below their lowest-scoring student. But Dr. Shechter was a truly honest man and drew the cut line where he thought it should be, even if his students were below it.

If we are observant, I believe God tries to teach us lessons and give us perspective. I remember slumping my way back to my apartment after failing another test. While waiting to cross High Street, I encountered a blind student, tapping his cane on the sidewalk and waiting for the "walk" sign to change and the bird sounds to chime, so he knew it was time to safely cross. Suddenly, my problems seemed ridiculously small. I had a minor hurdle to overcome. This student was bearing a huge burden for his whole life. What right did I have to feel sorry for myself? I thought God was teaching me a lesson, and I needed to appreciate my life situation.

I also believe God has a sense of humor. He teaches you lessons and reminds you in a comical way what is right and wrong. Several times over the next four years, I would be walking across campus in a bad or depressed mood, and out of nowhere, a blind person or a wheelchair-bound individual would appear. It seemed to happen every month or two. I would think, *Gotcha! God did it again. He caught me being self-centered.*

The Ohio State University has been a college football powerhouse for many decades. About every other Saturday in the fall, there were home football games in the "Horseshoe." A really foolish, but depressing feeling occurred when walking across campus on a Saturday morning to go to work in the chemistry lab all day, while everyone else was going to the game. I don't think God appreciates football.

5. Fear of Surgery and Flying

Surgery

I have had a number of surgeries in my life: two hernia repairs, broken arm (from the tree-climbing contest), two pilonidal cysts, wisdom teeth, and two colonoscopies. Surgery under anesthesia is a scary thing, and many people are absolutely terrified. My wife is a type-A person and likes to be in charge of most situations. So being "asleep" and getting cut open by a stranger is the last thing she wants. It doesn't matter if the doctors are extremely qualified or even world-class experts. She is not in charge, so she doesn't trust the outcome. Unfortunately, due to various medical conditions, she has also had a lot of surgeries under anesthesia: four laparoscopies, infertility surgery, hysterectomy, colonoscopy, parathyroid neck surgery, eye lens replacement, and recently, gallbladder removal. Pat's normal blood pressure is great at 120/80, and her heart rate is about seventy. Just prior to surgery, her blood pressure goes way up, to about 180/100 and her heart rate goes to about 150 beats per minute. It wouldn't get that high if she were sprinting down our driveway or riding an Exercycle full speed.

Typically before surgery, they give you a Valium or Demerol shot to calm you down. Even after the medicine, Pat's heart rate doesn't change, and she is still wide-awake and staring at the hospital staff with trepidation. I suspect this is probably a typical reaction for many people.

I'm more of a type-B person and want to be in charge of my life, but for a few minutes, I can let someone else lead an endeavor, whether it is in my business or my personal life. For whatever reason, when I go into surgery, I am fairly relaxed. I don't feel alone in the operating room. I feel a sense of calm and security. Surgery is almost a religious experience to me. I feel God is there with the doctors to make sure everything goes well. Whether this feeling is caused by my religious beliefs or the Demerol shot, I can't be sure. The Demerol certainly doesn't hurt, though!

Flying

Flying is another stressful activity, not unlike surgery. Many people are terrified of flying. Due to my job, I have typically taken about seventy flights a year for thirty years. I've been lucky to see much of the world on these trips. I certainly can't say flying is a religious experience, however. Going through security, waiting endlessly, airport and airplane food, and cramped seats make flying a real pain in the butt.

When I take my seat on a plane, I store my bag and take out something to read. However, most times I sleep for at least half the flight, particularly if they are morning flights and I had to get up early. Sometimes, I even sleep through the beverage service. If you know me, I never pass up free food and drink. So, for me to sleep through the service, I have to be tired.

Sometimes, while I am settling into my seat—usually a window— leaning my head against the wall and trying to go to sleep, passengers sit in my aisle and nervously look around. I can tell they have not flown often and hate to fly. Their head keeps turning, frantically looking around the plane. They usually stare at me, wondering why I'm sleeping when we are facing imminent death! I continue trying to fall asleep just to frustrate them more. This isn't nice, but I try not get involved with strangers.

While I feel protected in an operating room, I don't feel as secure flying if the plane starts to bounce. As I get older, I hate bouncing planes more and more.

I do feel God is protecting me in my travels, although I do *not* often achieve a complete state of calm. Maybe they should offer Demerol shots on plane flights; that would mellow out the passengers.

6. Infertility and Evan

After four years of marriage, Pat and I decided to have a baby. We felt we were emotionally and financially ready for the responsibility. We stopped "being careful" and tried, but with no success. Early in our marriage, we had developed a fondness for traveling, so we decided to go on romantic vacations to Miami, Bermuda, Cancun, Jamaica, and Las Vegas in the hope that different surroundings would let the magical event happen. We had fantastic times, but again, no luck conceiving.

After two years of trying, we realized we had a fertility problem. Pat and I were both tested extensively, and Pat was diagnosed with endometriosis. This was not a surprise, as her mother and grandmother had the same problem. Endometriosis is a disorder in which tissue that normally lines the inside of your uterus grows outside your uterus.

My non-medical interpretation is that the flow from her monthly period did not all come out, and some tissues remained and grew small tumors around her fallopian tubes and ovaries. In endometriosis, displaced endometrial tissue continues to act as it normally would: it thickens, breaks down, and bleeds with each menstrual cycle. And because this displaced tissue has no way to exit the body, it becomes trapped. Surrounding tissue can become irritated, eventually developing scar tissue and adhesions that bind organs together. These growths inhibit the normal flow of eggs and generally plug the conceiving apparatus. Some women have it so severe, the tumors wind around the outside of the intestines and choke off the flow of bodily waste and cause serious constipation. Pat had always had very heavy periods and terrible cramps. We had long known her female system was not in perfect working order.

Rather than going immediately to surgery, Dr. Brown, Pat's gynecologist, wanted to try less-invasive measures first. For months, the doctor put us on different sex schedules: every other day, every third day, every day. Pat monitored her temperature to determine when she ovulated and then we would have sex several times. One day, I remember getting a call at work and rushing home for a less than romantic lunchtime encounter. Pat was even on the fertility drug Clomid for a while. Still no pregnancy. We were then referred to the famous Dr. Moon Kim at the Ohio State University Hospital. After more examinations, including another laparoscopy, Dr. Kim determined she needed surgery.

Pat was scheduled to have major surgery in late February to remove her endometriosis and to examine her ovaries and fallopian tubes and clean them out if needed. We were supposed to stay away from each other (no sex!) the month before surgery. Usually, every Friday or Saturday night we would go to the movies or occasionally the orchestra. This particular weekend, the Ice Capades were in town, and we went to a nice dinner and the ice show, which was very good. When we arrived home, we had a weak moment and had intercourse. Those biological urges can be strong!

The day of surgery arrived, and about twenty minutes into the operation, Dr. Kim rushed back into the waiting room and said he thought Pat was about ten days pregnant. In all his surgeries, he had only seen this once before. The uterus had a different, pink color and was shiny. In 1984, with the technology available at the time, it was too early to get an accurate reading on a standard pregnancy test, but Dr. Kim was fairly certain. He said not to worry. The surgical team would give Pat extra oxygen and work fast to finish the surgery. Dr. Kim cleaned out the endometrial scar tissue as best he could and closed her up. Dr. Kim said at this stage, the baby would only be a few cells, encased in a protective sac and isolated from the mother. Therefore, the anesthetic would not bother the baby. Pat had Demerol before the surgery and would have morphine after the surgery for pain. Again, Dr. Kim said not to worry. Since so many drug addicts have had normal babies, they have lots of statistics that Demerol and morphine don't bother the baby or result in birth defects. At least one good thing has come out of drug addiction!

When Pat awoke, she asked how the surgery went, because she was afraid the news would be that she could not have any children. I said she was already pregnant! Forget the fancy vacations; it was the Ice Capades, or more likely the relaxation of not trying to have a baby.

When Dr. Kim, who emigrated from South Korea, came into the room, he bragged in broken English, "See, you came in with an infertility problem, and now you are leaving pregnant. Our program works very well!" We all laughed.

Since Pat had just had surgery and had an eight-inch scar on her lower belly, it was going to be a tricky pregnancy in regards to her stomach muscles. As the months went by, her stomach got bigger, and the scar was stretched to the limit. It ended up about fourteen inches long and about one inch wide. After giving birth, it did return to the eight-inch length.

In the first few months of pregnancy, Pat could just not gain weight. Her belly was getting bigger, and the baby appeared healthy on sonograms, but her legs and rest of her body were getting skinny. Our baby was acting like a tapeworm and absorbing much of Pat's nutrition. Dr. Chad Friedman, who was Dr. Kim's partner and did most of the deliveries, said, "Pat, you have to gain weight this month, or I'll put you in the hospital for intravenous feedings."

Pat had had enough of hospitals, so we found another solution. Every night we went to Dairy Queen, and Pat had a huge sundae. At the end of the month, she was up ten pounds (I was up five), and Dr. Friedman was happy, but told us to go back to a normal diet.

Pat developed high blood pressure during the pregnancy and had to spend much of the last few months on her left side, which somehow lowers the pressure.

We took the Lamaze classes to help Pat deal with the birthing pain, and we took classes on taking care of a new baby. I was an only child, had never babysat, and I had no young cousins or neighbors.

Babies and small children were totally foreign to me, so it helped me to put diapers on a doll and learn other techniques in the classes.

All along, Pat was convinced our baby would be a boy and that he was going to be big. Dr. Friedman did not know the sex, as the sonograms were inconclusive. He said the baby looked normal size. Pat has always had a nice figure and was 37-25-36 and 130 pounds prior to pregnancy. A few days before giving birth, she measured 42-42-42 and weighed 162 pounds. Her stomach was enormous. Since we knew the exact date of conception, and thus the due date, Dr. Friedman thought he should induce her labor on the due date if she did not go into labor on her own. Pat did not want a C-section, because she did not want her stomach cut again, so we were going to try a normal delivery.

It was Tuesday, November 6, 1984, the day Ronald Reagan was re-elected president. I went to vote on my way to the hospital. This was the due date. Dr. Friedman did not want Pat to go beyond term, so he started an IV of Pitocin, the drug used to induce labor. Right away, Pat was having big contractions. She was bucking like a bronco in the delivery chair. Lamaze breathing is a great technique, but after a few hours of hard contractions, Pat needed some pain medication. In Lamaze, the husband or companion breathes along with the expectant mother to re-enforce the technique and get the rhythm correct. After a few hours, Pat said, "Go breathe in your own face for a while. I need some painkillers." A key point in our Lamaze training is that the husband is told to ignore whatever his wife says in delivery. Women have been known to threaten to kill or castrate their husbands in their pain.

An anesthesiologist and his intern came in and gave Pat an epidural. Unfortunately, since Pat was lying on her left side to lower her blood pressure, the epidural only worked on one side. Being half numb was not very useful to control the pain or let you push evenly.

About two hours later, they came in again and gave her another epidural, which was perfect this time. Pat slept for over two hours, through huge contractions. You might ask how I knew this fact. When Dr. Friedman started to induce the labor in the morning, his staff had hooked up Pat to some sort of electric device that monitored the contractions. A strip of paper came out of the machine with a line graph of how hard the contraction was and, therefore, Pat's pain level. It occurred to me later that wives should really come with a machine like this, so we husbands could know if they are feeling well or are in some sort of pain. But in normal life, we have to figure this out the hard way.

So, Pat slept from about 4 to 6 p.m., and I finally got to eat my lunch. Then, about 6 p.m., Pat was fully dilated, and they told her to start pushing. She pushed on and off for about two hours but didn't make much progress. The baby was quite big, and Dr. Friedman tried forceps, with no luck. Then, he put a suction apparatus on the baby's head and tried to pull him out with that.

At one point, Dr. Friedman told Pat, "You are having a baby in the next half hour one way or another." They moved her from a birthing room to a delivery surgical room. All of a sudden, the hospital came alive with people. Nurses and residents were scrubbing up and getting ready for a C-section. It looked like they called SWAT to handle a terrorist, as there were people everywhere getting ready. Then, Pat and the nurse wanted to try one more time. Dr. Friedman had the baby's head with the forceps, Pat was going to push hard, and the nurse placed her arms on top of Pat's stomach, near her chest, and was going to push down the length of Pat's body to get extra force going toward the pelvis. On the count of three, all of them pushed, and out popped the baby's head. A little maneuvering to get one shoulder out and then out he came. He started to cry. Dr. Friedman cut the cord, and the nurse took him away for inspection.

Evan was huge—ten pounds two ounces—and perfectly healthy. Pat and I had received a miracle. Between Pat and me, the Ice Capades, Dr. Kim, Dr, Friedman, and God, we had our child.

Dr. Friedman spent another forty-five minutes stitching Pat back together. He had to cut Pat open quite a bit to get our son out. At one point, he was covered in blood, afterbirth, and goo. He shook his arms to the floor to get some of the slop off him arms and operating gown. He said, "I really need to change my gown, but don't want to take the time." At the end of the day, Dr. Friedman was as exhausted as Pat and more of a mess. So, at about 9:30 p.m., November 6, 1984, Floyd Evan Friedli was born. Pat always liked the name Evan, so we picked that in case he was a boy. We devised this weird family tradition of the same first names but different middle names. My father is Floyd Emmett Friedli, and he used his middle name. I am Floyd Ely Friedli, and I go by Floyd. Our son is Floyd Evan Friedli, and we call him Evan.

Just before I went home, I stopped by the nursery to see Evan one more time. As I approached the window where you could see all the babies, I heard someone say, "Look at that kid. He must be a month old." It was Evan who was drawing their attention. I was now a proud father and felt God had truly helped us conceive, lead us to the right doctors, and gave us a healthy baby boy.

7. Dad's Passing

My father, Floyd Emmett Friedli, was born poor on December 7, 1918, and grew up in a little town, Roscoe Village, during the Great Depression. His father, Grandpa Friedli, ran a water-powered flour mill in Roscoe. He had come over from Switzerland, and flour milling was the family business. Unfortunately, Grandpa Friedli did not own the flour mill. He just worked there, and it struggled as newer technologies took over. Dad's father died when Dad was seventeen. and his mother passed when he was twenty five. So, at a fairly early age, Dad and his brother, Francis, had to carry on alone. Frank went on to college and served in World War II. Dad attended a local business college and essentially was a self-taught accountant.

Note that Dad turned twenty-three on the day Pearl Harbor was attacked in 1941! Wasn't that a great birthday present! Dad was drafted, but rejected from the army for having flat feet. His feet were unusually flat. When he walked in the sand, his footprints were two ovals with little toe marks at the top. The army said he could not march long distances. Maybe someone was looking out for Dad! In retrospect, the army's rejection of him was odd, since one of his accounting friends was drafted and spent the entire war in Indianapolis, making out soldiers' paychecks. Dad certainly could have done that.

Emmett went on to be a successful businessman and was vice president, chief financial officer of the Edmont-Wilson Division of Becton Dickinson. He was a really good man, and the "last honest man," but that is another story. Since he grew up poor, he was always concerned about financial security. One of his life goals was that his son, me, would have a better life than he did. In a selfish way, I thought this was a very good goal! Dad was very frugal, but not cheap, and was good at accumulating money and making it grow in the stock market. He never wanted to be poor again; he wanted enough money to withstand any calamity or downturn in the economy.

Dad didn't get much exercise and was rather sedentary in his lifestyle and job. However, he did love to work in our yard—mowing grass, trimming bushes, planting flowers, growing vegetables and grapes, and so on. Unfortunately, he only worked in the yard on Saturdays, and one day a week is not enough exercise.

Eventually, the sedentary lifestyle and many years of smoking two packs of Chesterfields a day caught up with him, and he had a double by-pass at age sixty-four. He recovered well, quit smoking for good this time, and lived another twenty years.

At about age eighty-three, he started having headaches and was diagnosed with brain cancer. Somehow, they could tell that the cancer in his brain was not the primary cancer but a secondary one, which had come from somewhere else in his body. He had no other symptoms, but after much searching, they found a small spot of cancer way back on his tongue; that was the primary cancer. I never understood how they knew which was primary and which was the metastasized cancer. Cancer on the back of the tongue is common for smokers who have a drink or two every day. After ruling out some gruesome operations due to his age, he received a number of radiation treatments on his head and neck. The treatments shrunk the tumors and relieved his headaches, but they did not eliminate or cure the cancer.

My parents' doctor was an old Korean doctor who had immigrated to the United States thirty years ago. Dr. Kim (a different Dr. Kim than previously mentioned) was a great doctor and gave my parents a lot of personal attention. He was open and honest, and told me that Dad's heart was failing and his heart would give out before the cancer got him. While not good news, it was a blessing in reality. By the time he was eighty-four, Dad needed oxygen, because his heart was getting weaker.

Dad had been getting weaker, and I went to visit Mom and Dad for a few hours almost every week. They still lived in Coshocton, Ohio, while Pat and I lived in Dublin, Ohio, about ninety miles away. For months throughout the spring, Dad was getting more frail but then seemed to rally a little. One Saturday, Pat, Evan, and I had been planning to visit my parents, when we thought, *"Dad seems to be getting better, maybe we could skip this visit."* Fortunately, by the grace of God, we decided to go anyway. We had a great visit, and Dad and I even went over his tax return, which his lawyer had prepared for him. Dad's mind was sharp to the end. He asked specific questions and knew all the details. The next day, Sunday, April 6, I received a call from the hospital that Dad had passed away. He was having trouble breathing, and Mom called the squad. He died as he got to the hospital, at eighty-four and a half, after a good, long life.

In looking as his death, it was perfect, as if someone higher had planned it. Dad went before the pain got too bad, he died the day after our last visit, and he did not die at their home: he died at the hospital. I think it would have been a little creepy if he died in the apartment and my mother continued to live there. I truly believe a higher power organized his passing.

Unfortunately, Mom's recent death was not as easy. Mom had been a teacher for five years and a homemaker the rest of her life. While she loved to work in the yard with Dad, her hobby was reading and, thus, was also very sedentary. She died two weeks short of being ninety, and her health had been failing for about a year, more quickly the last six months. Mom had no particular disease; she was just wearing out. Both her mind and body were declining. She could hardly walk and had the beginnings of Alzheimer's or dementia. She lived in assisted living for a number of years, and sometimes she got confused. She would think she was back in college, living in the dormitory, and her parents were coming to pick her up for the summer. I would think, but usually not say, *"Mom, they died over fifty years ago! Grandpa and Grandma Ely are not coming back."*

I knew during her visit to our house last Christmas that this likely was her last visit. Mom was much weaker, and it was all my wife and I could do to get her dressed and take care of her bathroom duties.

Most of her life, Mom had been a good eater, but in January, she started to lose her appetite. She had gone to the hospital twice after collapsing due to extremely low blood pressure and low blood sugar from not eating enough. The last two months, she was under the care of Hospice, who did a great job of picking up her spirits and taking care of her.

When Mom became totally bedridden in June and could no longer eat or drink, we knew the end was near. Pat and I and our son and his wife came over for a last visit. Pat and I stayed in her apartment for the weekend. We said our good-byes on Sunday morning, and within an hour, she was either asleep or in a coma. Mom passed Monday morning, and I literally saw her last two breaths. Her breathing had been faster all morning, which means the body is fighting until the end. I went down the hall for a few minutes to run an errand. When I came back and checked on her, Mom gasped a loud breath. This is another sign that the end is very close, but the gasping can go on for hours. About a minute later, Mom gasped her last breath and was gone.

While Mom's death was slower and more difficult for her to endure and us to watch, I believe it had a purpose. I got to see how precious life is, I got to see how the body struggles to the end, and I had time to reflect on my relationship with my parents. Fortunately, Mom lasted long enough for the family to visit and say our good-byes, and I was there until the end. By luck or design from above, the quicker, easier, death, Dad's, came first, which helped give me the strength to watch Mom's slower passing. It was very tough, but I believe it means a lot to the sick person and to you to be there at the end.

8. Pain in the Neck—
Spasmodic Torticollis

In January 2007, I noticed that it was difficult for me to turn my head to the right. My wife and a friend noticed that my head shook slightly. I could not feel it, but they noticed a definite tremor. My annual physical had been scheduled for the end of January, but my doctor got seriously ill, and my physical was delayed until early April. I described by symptoms to my doctor and he x-rayed my neck. He saw nothing unusual or any sign of injury. Of course, during my physical my head did not shake, so he said we should just watch wait and see if the symptoms continued.

The more my wife noticed my shaking head, the more I was worried that I had Parkinson's disease. I checked the Internet, but my symptoms weren't quite right. In late April, I brought the X-rays to my regular chiropractor, and he adjusted my neck, which made it feel better and gave it a little more mobility for a while. But he didn't have a diagnosis. In May, I saw another chiropractor, and on the second visit, he said, "I think you have spasmodic torticollis and should see a neurologist." He contacted a local neurology office that treats this sort of thing, but it took six weeks to get into see the neurologist. Apparently, there are large numbers of people who have various neurological problems. During the months that passed, my neck got stiffer and harder to turn to the right. I was noticing that at times I could feel my head shaking.

After several tests by the neurologist, including a MRI to make sure I didn't have a brain tumor, I was officially diagnosed with spasmodic torticollis, also known as cervical dystonia. This is a fairly rare disease, affecting about one hundred thousand people in the United States. "Torticollis" means tilting of the head, so spasmodic torticollis is the involuntary tilting or turning of the head. Once I knew the weird name of my disease, I found many Internet sites and a lot of information about different treatments. I also joined the National Spasmodic Torticollis Association and get their newsletter. There are also numerous support groups around the country to help patients and families cope with the problems and lifestyle changes that occur. Spasmodic torticollis is known as a nuisance disease, meaning it causes you discomfort or problems but is not dangerous or terminal. It is also incurable, but treatable. I take Botox injections in several neck muscles every three months to weaken the overactive nerves and muscles and make it easier to me to keep my head somewhat straight and able to turn to the right when needed.

After about one and a half years with my first neurologist, I switched to a more experienced neurologist in Toledo. It is worth the two-and-a-half-hour drive every three months to see a true expert. The Toledo doctor has treated about one thousand patients like me from all over the world.

The Botox injections I take are just like the ones people get to remove wrinkles in their face, except they use a lower dose on your face. Botox is a neurotoxin that paralyzes or weakens the nerves that operate nearby muscles. In your face, the Botox causes your face muscles to relax and flattens out wrinkles. The higher dose I get in my neck weakens the "pulling" muscles that turn my head to the left. In this way, the opposite muscles that turn my head to the right have a better chance of balancing the overactive muscles so that I can hold my head a little straighter. I still have to think about turning my head to the right, but with the shots, it is easier. Botox only lasts about three to four months before the effect wears off. Plus, some people even develop an immunity to it and then Botox no longer works for them. To lessen the chance of immunity, the doctor gives a series of shots every three months at the minimum dose the patient says gives them a reasonable lifestyle. After the injections, it takes two to three weeks to get the maximum effect. Then, you can feel the effect start to slowly weaken at about the nine-week mark. Unless they find a cure, I will take the shots the rest of my life. No other medicines or pills work very well for my disease. In really severe cases, some nerve medicines are combined with Botox.

Fortunately, my spasmodic torticollis is fairly mild. Many people end up on disability or have limited activities. I can still do almost all my previous activities. As my neck gets tight and stiff, I stretch it out and do the physical therapy that loosens it up. A few Tylenol or ibuprofen are also my friends. Before I play golf, I take one or two tablets to head off the stiffness and pain. After nine holes, I usually take one or two more. Overall, my disease is livable.

I am not sure what other people see or think of me, since few people say anything about my appearance. But I assume I occasionally look a little strange with my head turned in an odd position. When I am on a sales call, I try to sit so the clients are slightly to my left, which is the direction my head naturally turns now. They probably don't notice much if the meeting is less than an hour. If I have longer, internal, company meetings, I try to sit so I am looking slightly right. This is more work, but stretches the "bad" muscles and may relax them.

One of the most difficult, but critical, tasks affected was driving the car. Until the treatment dosage and injection locations were optimized, driving was very tiring.

Getting my picture taken is a problem. If I sit so I can look slightly left, I may take a usable picture. If someone takes a picture where I need to look to the right and hold that pose, I will end up looking really deformed.

After experiencing several months of moderate depression, I eventually accepted the hand I had been dealt. I wondered if God was punishing me for my family's financial success, for being too materialistic, for being too self-centered. I certainly don't believe he is punishing me; it was just a random problem that happened to hit me.

However, I think God is using this random disease to open my eyes and let me see the less fortunate people around me.

It is as if my vision has improved in a nontraditional way. A few years before my disease, as I went about my life running errands or traveling on business, I would run into individuals with handicaps or people who had various medical or financial problems. I would stay in my own cocoon and hardly see them. I might glance over and see them briefly and think, *That's too bad,* but I might not see them at all! Now, my powers of observation are keen. I see people with various afflictions—walk with a limp, have deformities, appear developmentally disabled, have scars from serious injuries, and so on. Now, I believe I can empathize with these people. I see them rather than see through them. I now see them as real people, going about their lives under the circumstances they were given. They might be struggling to walk through a grocery store. They might be trying to figure out the signs in an airport. They might even be concerned if people are staring at them. I hope I am not doing that and making them uncomfortable.

As I observe their plight in life, suddenly my problems are again put in perspective.

9. All God's Creatures

If you are a skeptic as to whether there is a God, I suggest just looking around at the beautiful plants and animals that make up this world. They cannot just be a coincidence or just survival of the fittest. A beautiful coloring of a tiger or giraffe cannot really help their survival that much.

I am a scientist and believe in evolution, but it appears that evolution had a purpose. There seem to be an endless number of plants and animals in the world. In the animal kingdom, there are bacteria, amoeba, worms, bugs, fish, birds, lizards, mammals, and finally, man. Why do we need this much variety? Maybe variety leads to a durable system that can continue on as climates and situations change. The beauty in the plant and animal world are not a coincidence. Why does a jungle parrot need such bright colors?

I believe God gave us pets to take care of, enjoy, and keep us company. A cat or dog can really add a huge amount of joy to a person or family. Taking care of them teaches you responsibility and love. It has been shown that pets keep older, widowed men and women more active, happier, and they live longer.

I believe that all forms of life that come in contact with you for long periods of time are a gift from God. God gave me my wife, Pat, and my son, Evan. God has given us a number of wonderful cats. We prefer cats to dogs, because they are cute and easier to take care of. Cats don't have to be walked and can be left alone for a few days to fend for themselves with just a bowl of food, some water, and a litter box. Our favorite breed is Turkish Angora. These cats are very friendly and love to spend a lot of time with you. They are like dogs in a cat's body. We had Snowy, a deaf, white male for fifteen years; Snowball, a hearing, white male for almost seventeen years; and now we have a brother and sister, Cleopatra and Thunder, a smoke-colored female and another while male.

I believe that when you pick out a puppy or kitten from a breeder, pet store, shelter, or friend, you don't really pick it out. God gives you that animal to take care of. You have a big responsibility to give that animal a good life.

Therefore, I believe God gave me a solemn job. My job is to take care of Pat, Evan, and our cats—to give them the best life possible and to protect them as long as I am mentally and physically able to do so. My job is not just to work for my employer to increase their profits. My real job is to bring home money to take care of my family. I may do that by increasing the profits for my company, but that is not the main focus.

The implications to the various aspects of this job are immense. For one, we should avoid divorce at all costs. We have a responsibility to make the marriage work, make your partner happy, love them, take care of them, and so on.

For children, we must teach them to be useful in society, to be able to take care of themselves as they get older, to accept responsibility at appropriate times, not to abuse them, to love them, and so on.

Even for pets, the responsibility is large. They must be trained, fed, given shelter, loved, protected from harm, and given adequate medical attention. One cannot just abandon an animal or get rid of it when you move or no longer find it interesting. God gave you that animal to take care of for its entire life.

It was about 1986, and I had a particularly bad day at work, I drove in the driveway of our first house, and looking out the family room window were two-year-old Evan and our first cat, Snowy. They were eagerly waiting for me to come home to be with them. Seeing their faces showed me the true meaning of life: family. The problems at work instantly became insignificant, and I spent the next few hours playing with Evan and Snowy.

Legos are of one of the greatest toys ever invented. From the time Evan was about two until he entered high school, we would spend a few nights a week building something with Legos. I find there are few things as relaxing as playing with your child and putting those little building blocks together. By the time Evan was fourteen, we had built an entire city on two four-by-eight-foot sheets of plywood. The city had a train, airport, shopping mall, police station, fire station, open-air shopping area, bank, space shuttle launch area, and so on. If your blood pressure is getting high, go buy a Lego kit and put something together. Playing with or petting your cat or dog also lowers your blood pressure. But I recommend keeping them away from the Lego set-up. They will wreck it and raise your blood pressure!

10. And the Trumpet Shall Sound

God works in mysterious ways. I don't believe in destiny or predetermination. I believe we make our own choices, and we make decisions every day that affect our lives today and sometimes far into the future. I do believe that God affects our lives. He might nudge your thinking in a certain direction. He might present you with an opportunity you can take or reject. He might occasionally open doors you can either walk through or ignore. He might show you different things that can influence you to take a certain path, but you still must make a choice and take one path or another.

Music is a gift from God. The fact that civilization has created beautiful music of all types is another proof of the existence of God. Music is a luxury and not a necessity to survival. Musical talent is certainly a gift. Some people have it, and some don't; most, like me, have a little talent. But we can all enjoy playing or listening to music.

When I was about ten years old, I would occasionally stay up late and watch *The Tonight Show Starring Johnny Carson*. I would see Doc Severinsen lead the *Tonight Show* band and play the trumpet. Ever since then, I wanted to play the trumpet. In sixth grade, you took a flutaphone class to teach you basic music theory and see if you had any music talent. The flutaphone was a boring instrument, and I showed limited interest and ability on it. However, when the band director came around and asked kids if they wanted to be in the band and choose an instrument, I was definitely excited. The band director suggested I try the saxophone, since my teeth were a little crooked and I had an overbite. Fortunately, my mom and I insisted I wanted to try the trumpet. While certainly not a child prodigy, I practiced and made some decent progress on the instrument. I was the best in our little elementary school.

I continued on through middle school and high school. I took lessons and made progress and was second chair trumpet most of high school. The first chair, Dave, was slightly better than I was, and we became best friends. There were two highlights to my high school playing. Dave and I played Vivaldi's "Concerto for Two Trumpets" with the high school band, and we played it really well. From seventh grade though twelfth grade, I entered the annual OMEA (Ohio Music Educators Association) contests. Sometimes I did well; other times, I struggled. In seventh and eighth grades, we were allowed to use the music, where in high school contests, you had to memorize your piece. In my first contest in seventh grade, I got so nervous I got lost in the music and had to stop, to the judge's dismay. "How can you get lost? You're looking right at the music!" I ended up playing pretty well, and the judge gave me a break and a good score.

Typically, when I played a solo in public during junior high and high school, I would get really nervous. I would be shaking, have either no saliva or way too much, and I would usually have a least one episode of diarrhea before performing. It's really hard to have good breath support and blow hard when you are concerned about having an accident in your shorts. But I would usually prevail and keep my physical limitations in control and perform adequately.

My second high school playing highlight was in my senior year in the OMEA contest. I played "The Debutante" and received the highest rating. I always had good technique but lacked tone and style. Therefore, I chose the "Debutante," because it was quite difficult and had many fast notes, but it didn't require a beautiful sound or good styling.

The reality of most musical instruments is that if you are reasonably intelligent and practice hard, you can learn almost any of them and play decently. I don't mean you will play fantastically or impress large numbers of people, but you can sound good, hit the correct notes, and show people you know what you are doing. That was and is my playing. I was not given much natural musical talent. I don't have a great feel for different types of music. I don't have a good ear to make sure I always play in tune. More important for the trumpet, I don't have a large lung capacity to really blow a lot of air through the horn. Therefore, I had a hard time getting a good tone and certainly was not any good at hitting high notes. But I loved to play. I loved the sound of the trumpet, I loved the feeling of blowing the air through the trumpet and making music. Playing the trumpet is an emotional experience. You become one with your instrument. The act of breathing deeply and blowing hard through the trumpet bonds you to the trumpet while you are playing a piece. Over time, I have worked on my breathing and my tone and now get a much better sound. Now, I prefer to play and listen to slow, lyrical music, where a good tone and style are required, as opposed to a hard, technical part with lots of fast notes.

Dad always loved to play the piano and eventually bought a Conn organ. Buying the organ was one of the luxuries he allowed himself. While Dad loved to play the piano and organ, he was like me, in that he had only a small amount of musical talent but made up for it with desire and practicing. As I prepared for the high school OMEA Contests, Dad would learn the piano accompaniment and work with me. This was a tremendous advantage for me, plus it was something Dad and I could do together and really enjoy. Dad would not actually accompany me at the contest; a good high school student would also learn the piece. Dad did not feel he was good enough to take on the actual performance.

My wife has real musical talent. It ran in both sides of the family. Her paternal grandmother could play the piano by ear very well, without ever taking lessons. Her father was an accomplished violinist and had a chance to play in the Cleveland orchestra. Pat has two cousins on her father's side who are professors of music (saxophone and trombone). Pat's mother did not appear to be overly musical, but her sister Florence was an excellent piano player.

Pat was really a child prodigy and could play the piano from the day she sat down in front of it. She studied at Baldwin Wallace College while she was in high school and played and practiced a lot.

Even people with talent need to practice a lot. They just get better much faster. People with real talent keep getting better and don't reach a plateau as early as the rest of us. I practiced and only slowly made any progress.

In college, Pat could "sight read" music better than all the college professors at Wooster. Pat's limitation was her hands were not very big. They were fairly big for a woman but not compared to most male piano majors, who have hands like a basketball players. If Pat had big hands, she would probably be a concert pianist or at least an accompanist for a famous singer. If her hands had been big and she became famous, we might never have met and married.

Our son, Evan, heard me playing the trumpet often when he was a little boy. I must have done something right. When he had the choice to join the sixth-grade band at Wyandotte Elementary School, he definitely wanted to play in the band and chose the trumpet. I gave him the trumpet I played in high school, which was much better than any beginning trumpet. He immediately could make a decent sound, and he was one of the better players in his elementary school. Pat and I alternated with giving him lessons, so he made good progress. Evan was never one to practice boring trumpet etudes. Lip flexibility exercises, tonguing studies, chromatic scales, and such were not his thing. He just wanted to play real music. Through middle school, Evan played fairly well and received top scores in middle-school music contests.

At that time, Dublin Coffman High School had one of the top-five marching bands in the state of Ohio. This was due to three factors. First, the community was fairly wealthy, and the students were from educated successful parents. Second, the high school was large, so there were many students from which to choose. Third, the band was lead by Dr. Keller. He was a tremendous trombone player, had a PhD in music from The Ohio State University, and played in The Ohio State University Marching Band, known as "the best damn band in the land." And he was a very strict teacher. Fortunately, my son adjusted to Dr. Keller's authoritarian approach and liked the hard work and structure of the band. It was almost like being in the army.

During the fall football season, the band practiced several hours a day and prepared an elaborate show that included solos by several of the top musicians in the band. The turning point in Evan's trumpet playing came his freshman year, during the first halftime show. Adam, the first-chair trumpet and a senior, came forward from the band and had an interesting solo, with the band playing the accompaniment. Suddenly, Evan wanted to be that soloist. He decided that when he was a senior, he wanted that year's solo.

Evan was now a serious player. He played a lot in school and learned a lot from the older trumpet players and from Dr. Keller. Pat and I still taught him every week or so. When the January OMEA music contests came around, Evan decided he wanted to play a Class A solo. A freshman almost never played Class A solos, as they are too difficult. Evan insisted and played Goedicke's "Etude." This was a difficult piece and, for most players, required double tonguing. He practiced the piece with me and played it at home a number of times with Pat as the accompanist. Having your mother as the piano player has some obvious disadvantages, however, it was really a great advantage.

In the contest performance, Evan did very well, but received a 2 rating, or excellent. The rating system for the OMEA has always been 1-superior, 2-excellent, 3-fair, 4-needs improvement, and 5-poor. Superior ratings are extremely difficult to get. Typically, out of thirty trumpet players in a district, they rated only two or three as superior. Evan's piece was a little too long for his endurance as a freshman, and he was wearing out the last few lines. He was not discouraged and kept on working. But Evan had impressed Adam, the first-chair trumpet, whom Evan wanted to emulate.

There were many fine trumpet players in Dublin Coffman. The band was so large that they had three concert bands. Evan practiced the audition pieces hard with my help and kept moving up in the bands, and he kept doing the contests. By his junior year, he was third chair in the top band. When the OMEA contest came around, he chose "Adagio and Allegro" by Barat. This is my wife's favorite trumpet piece. I played it in college, with her as my pianist. The "Adagio" part is a very beautiful solo. By now, we had purchased Evan the latest professional trumpet. Evan had a beautiful, full sound on the trumpet. His tone was excellent. He had a natural lip vibrato, which he learned and developed himself. He played the piece perfectly and easily received a superior rating. I heard most of the trumpet players that day, and the two best were Evan and a senior from another school, who was going to be a trumpet major in college.

Senior year came around, and it was marching band season. I don't know if it was luck or planning by Dr. Keller, but for the trumpet solo, he chose "Channel One Suite." This piece had a long, three-part trumpet solo that was very lyrical. As he had planned his freshman year, Evan won the solo. We first heard it parents' night in August band camp. This was the next to last day of weeklong band camp, when they previewed the band's contest show to the parents. It was really a rehearsal, since they would stop and correct mistakes as the occurred. When the second piece began, Evan stepped forward and began to play his solo. Pat and I almost fell down. Suddenly, this beautiful trumpet music was coming from our son. His sound was amazing. His tone could match that of any professional player I have heard. Dr. Keller stopped the piece after about fifteen seconds not due to Evan, but there were problems with the band accompaniment and the marching behind Evan. They probably did this ten times, until everything was right. But each time, Evan's solo was great. He played it again and again. I have no idea how he had the endurance to keep playing it and playing it well each time.

Throughout the fall, Evan performed that solo in public about twenty times—at every football game, at several fund raisers for the parents and community, and for about five marching band contests. It was always perfect. Even when standing in front of six thousand people at home football games, Evan did not appear nervous.

Seeing your children engaged in an activity they really enjoy and seeing them perform in a sporting or musical event is one of the greatest parts of being a parent. You hope they do well and have fun. If they don't, you have to help them recover from the game-ending error they had in baseball, the missed notes in a musical performance, or the forgotten lines in a play.

Watching our son play the trumpet well in front of large groups of people was one of the most rewarding times of my life. Experiencing his playing was truly a gift from God, for which I can never thank him. It was also a gift from Dr. Keller, the band director who chose him.

He was given his mother's talent. Who knows whether this was strictly genetics or a gift from God. While I practiced a lot and had reasonable technique, Evan had what you could not buy or practice enough to perfect. He had a great sound, great ear to play in tune, a natural lip vibrato, and a real feeling for the music, particularly lyrical pieces and jazz. He had the additional quality that he did not get nervous performing in front of large groups of people. He played extremely well even, though he was an undeveloped talent. He had not gone through all the exercises or music literature most players do to perfect their technique.

For three years, Evan took lessons in college from a fine jazz trumpet teacher and enjoyed it. He also realized, as I had, that taking music lessons in college is a fun way to get credit. I highly recommend this activity for anyone starting college. It's much better to play your instrument or sing for credit than sit through another boring history class. However, it is not an easy A, because most colleges have very high musical standards.

Our son is a realist, like his grandfather Friedli. In college, besides his studies, Evan was getting pulled between baseball, trumpet, weight lifting, and golf. He did all very well, but after three years, decided he wanted to do just two extremely well. Since he thought he had gone as far as he could in baseball and had already been very successful on the trumpet, he wanted to pursue bodybuilding and golf as his hobbies. Parents have to let their children do what interests them, not you. Hopefully, someday he will take up the trumpet again.

God works in strange ways, but maybe in brilliant ways. I had the desire, but not the God-given talent, while Evan had considerable talent but not the burning desire. Had I Evan's talent, I would have been a music major in college. If he had my desire, he probably would have been a music major in college. The net result is had we been music majors, we would be starving trumpet players right now. Actually playing an instrument for a living is very difficult. Many people have talent and play very well. However, there are very few jobs out there. For a typical opening in an orchestra, four hundred people will show up for the position. All play decently. Probably at least fifty would do a fine job. And the top ten are so close that it is almost impossible to make a choice.

For many years as an adult, I practiced and played the trumpet. I could not really find a group to play with and did not look too hard, since I was not sure I was good enough.

A local amateur orchestra (Cardinal Health) had a need for a trumpet player, and I joined. It was, and is, tremendous fun. After a few years, five of us formed the Dublin Brass Quintet, and we play at various charitable and sometimes paying events like weddings around Columbus. We play a lot in the local Catholic churches for Christmas and Easter. We get paid for these performances, and I feel guilty taking money from a church to play. For ego's sake, I still take the money, because I can always give it back as a donation.

While I believe God does watch over me, he certainly does not protect me from missing notes or making mistakes, even when playing at a church service. Playing a piece correctly, with some musical style, is strictly up to me. Practice and controlling my nerves are what is needed here. Praying for a good performance does not and should not work. I do usually wear my lucky socks, however, and they seem to help. I still get nervous when playing solos in public, but now only slightly nervous and, fortunately, no more diarrhea.

11. Everyone Needs a Good Firing

I had a rewarding career as a research chemist and manager in the surfactants field. After being hired in 1978 by Ashland Chemical, my division was sold several times and became Sherex Chemical, Witco, Goldschmidt, and finally Degussa. I had good bosses, and we did very interesting work. We were not curing cancer, but we were taking beef fat, coconut oil, and soybean oil and making fabric softeners, hair conditioners, iron ore purification chemicals, road-building chemicals, detergents, and other useful materials from these natural feedstocks. I was able to publish a few scientific papers and received seven patents on my work. My best work was actually kept secret as process improvements in our manufacturing. I was promoted into middle management fairly early in my career but was never chosen into the executive ranks, as I lacked several key personality characteristics. Being viewed as too nice and not having obvious business savvy can hurt your career. And not being good at playing the political game, I was passed over for several promotions. But I had no regrets, since the work was interesting, and the chemists I supervised were great people and good scientists.

While my research group had been through several company sales and transitions in twenty-three years, we never were required to move from Dublin, Ohio, nor did I get laid off. Not getting let go or being asked to move is unbelievable, really incredible. But finally, under Degussa, they wanted to relocate our lab and office to Richmond, Virginia, where they had another manufacturing plant. At that time, I was not thrilled with current management, and my wife and I didn't want to move. Evan was a junior in high school, Pat's and my parents were getting elderly, and we just didn't want to move. So, after much thought, I chose to leave the company. They were pressuring me to move, because they needed my expertise. While generally I am quiet and go with the flow, I got rather vocal at that time with the division president, saying the director of research and development (R&D) and the vice president of marketing didn't have half the knowledge I did. I said I would not move unless they basically doubled my salary and promoted me several levels. Division presidents don't like smart asses, so in a few days, I was asked to leave the company immediately. Even if people were not taking the transfer, Degussa had guaranteed our jobs until August of 2002, but suddenly, in December 2001, they threw me out the door. I learned several lessons from this. First, everyone is replaceable, and even if you are not, they may get rid of you anyway. The second lesson is do not be afraid to contact a lawyer if you think you have been treated unfairly. Very quickly, my lawyer got me the full severance package and reinstated my bonus for the year.

I incorporated myself and started Friedli Chemical Consulting. As I was putting together my brochures and looking for clients, I got a double interview at Akzo Nobel. One of my previous bosses, Jeanenne, was now in marketing at Akzo Nobel, and I knew Dale, the director of research and development. We had met at an industry conference about nine years earlier, when Dale was chairing a technical session. One of my chemists was going to give a talk on fabric softeners in Dale's session, but she was involved in a car accident with her sister. Nancy was not hurt but wanted to stay with her sister to make sure she was all right. Fortunately, everyone was fine. However, Nancy was going to miss her speech and asked me to either tell Dale she could not make it, or I could give her talk. I briefly looked at her slides and thought I could fake her speech since she worked for me, and I knew about her project. I told Dale of the situation, and he was glad I was willing to freelance her technical talk. While I get nervous playing the trumpet, I do not get very nervous giving a speech in front of large number of people if I know the subject matter. Well, I gave Nancy's talk in my own words, and the audience and Dale were impressed. I believe God had opened a door for me, and I was lucky enough to walk through it. This choice would have unintended consequences years in the future, because it resulted in the interview at Akzo Nobel.

My interview at Akzo Nobel was a double interview. Dale wanted a consultant to help with some technical issues; they also had an opening for a new salesperson to cover their largest customer, Procter & Gamble. I had worked with Procter & Gamble for my entire career on numerous projects. Both parts of the interview went well, and Dale offered me the choice of jobs. While the technical part was right up my knowledge base, I chose to take the sales job, covering Procter and Gamble, and become a full-time Akzo Nobel employee. Again, it appeared that God had opened a door, and I had about ten seconds to decide the next few years of my life. Fortunately, I chose correctly. The P&G sales job fit me well, and I enjoyed it. I didn't have to move, as P&G was only about a ninety-minute drive from my house. I typically went there one or two days per week.

In the nine years I have worked at Akzo Nobel, we have reorganized the sales force several times, and I now have a number of different clients around the country. I work from my home and travel about three days a week, typically flying to New York, Chicago, Milwaukee, or Atlanta. I've been able to contribute well to our business, work reasonable hours, and make more money than I have ever made.

In retrospect, getting fired from my previous company was one of the greatest things that ever happened to me. My wife and I look back at the chain of events, the decisions we made, and say, "Whew! We really got lucky here." Luck or help from above?

Most of my old research group at Degussa did not move to Richmond but stayed in Columbus. They all found other jobs and are doing fine now. It was traumatic at first, since many of us had been there for over twenty years, but there is life after your current job.

If you lose your job, and the economy is not totally in the dumps, you can probably find a new job or start a business. You may end up in a better situation or at least get a change of scenery and new experiences. Try to stay calm, and I wish you the best of luck.

12. Bad Luck Comes in Threes

Pat has always said bad luck comes in threes. I don't know where this saying came from, but I won't disagree now.

Bad Luck Part 1—Lightning

It was late June 2009, Friday before Father's Day, and a terrible thunderstorm came through our area about 5 a.m. Suddenly, Pat and I heard loud thunder cracks. They got louder and louder, and we both thought we were going to get hit. Crack! Our whole house shook, and we knew lightning had hit our house. We don't have a regular doorbell; our two main entrances are connected to our house stereo system. When the front door rings, it plays the Big Ben chimes through the house sound system, while the side door, where Pat's pianos students come in, plays Chopin's "Polonaise." The lightning hit the stereo system and doorbell, resulting in Chopin's "Polonaise" playing at full volume throughout the house. The doorbell ring is about ten seconds of "Polonaise," which played again, and again, and again.

So, Pat and I ran around the house to see what damage we had and if the house was on fire. I couldn't think straight, with Chopin's "Polonaise" playing. I even ran outside in the rain in my underwear and looked up at the chimneys, expecting them to be knocked off the house and possibly see the roof on fire. Surprisingly, everything looked normal, at least in the dark. Then, I ran downstairs to shut off the doorbell, and I couldn't get the machine to do anything; it just kept playing. I then ran upstairs to the pull-down staircase to the attic and went up to see if the roof and attic were on fire.

Fortunately, everything seemed fine. After about fifteen minutes, Pat said, "I smell gas." I was skeptical at first, thinking we just smelled something left over from the lightning. But she insisted, and I finally agreed with her, and she called Columbia Gas. The lady on the phone said, "Don't turn on anything electrical, including light switches." Great, I had been running around the house, turning on light switches everywhere! Some worked, some didn't. Within about twenty minutes, a Columbia Gas man showed up with a gas detector and started going around the house, looking for a leak. He definitely detected gas, and we shut off the lines in the basement to everything in the house.

We also called our builder, and he called our electrician, who came out about 6:30 a.m. He finally got that crazy doorbell to stop playing Chopin. Our bedroom lights didn't work, and a number of other items were fried.

For the moment, the house was all right, and we were safe. The gas guy said that in new homes, they use this flexible metal gas pipe covered in yellow plastic. If your house is hit with lightning and your gas lines are not grounded, it blows a small hole in them and leaks gas. When we built our house, it was not code to ground the gas lines. But after a number of houses burned down around the country, they have since changed the code.

The lightning had blown holes in our gas lines. Over the next month, we had two gas leak companies and our plumber come out to try to find the leak. The leaking line would be in the walls, and we didn't want to tear up the drywall in the whole house looking for the leak. All the lines were pressured tested with air, and two were found to be bad. Still, we didn't know where in the walls the leaks were. The lines tend to blow out near a bend in the pipe or a pipe near another metal item, like a water pipe or an electrical box. An adjuster from Nationwide Insurance came out several times, doing inspections and estimating what would need to be repaired. Finally, our plumber put air pressure on the various lines, and he and Pat listened in the walls for a "hissing" sound. I had no idea where the sound was coming from, but Pat and the plumber could tell to within a foot of where it was. Small holes were cut in the drywall, and, fortunately, the leaks were found and repaired. In all, we lost part of the house stereo, two computers, several TVs, and smaller items to a total of about $10,000. Nationwide Insurance was very helpful and covered everything but the deductible. We were extremely lucky that our house did not burn down and no one was hurt. So, after about six weeks, we were about back to normal. Someone had protected us.

Bad Luck Part 2—Car Wreck

My son inherited a passion for sports cars, like his father. He was very spoiled, and we got him a Camaro with three hundred horsepower when he was a new driver. Fortunately, he is a very careful person by nature and does not take a lot of risks with his body. From the moment he started to drive, he was excellent. He paid attention and had real skill with the car. He can back up and park with the best. I never worried about him causing an accident. I only worried he would get lost, because he has his mother's sense of direction.

Early in his driving, I realized what was important. Our neighbor's daughter, Kathy, who was a straight-A student, wrecked her car within a few months of starting to drive. I looked at Evan and realized it was better to have a B student who could drive well than a straight-A student who might not live to adulthood.

Evan did like lots of horsepower and drag racing. He did the drag racing at legitimate racetracks and not on the street—as far as I know. He and his buddies worked on the car, getting it up to about three hundred fifty horsepower. Then, Evan started saving his money and taking it to a garage for better air intake, a more-efficient belt system, a roll cage, headers, stronger camshaft, new gears and rear end, and finally, a supercharger. Over about seven years, his car climbed to four hundred horsepower, five hundred horsepower, and about six hundred ten horsepower. Several times each year, he would take it to the drag strip and race it against other similar cars. He would do pretty well. The smartest purchase he made was the roll cage to protect the driver and passengers in the event of a serious accident.

Evan would only drive his "baby" on clear days with no chance of rain. Otherwise, he would drive his old Jeep.

As was usual on a nice summer Friday night, Evan would come by our house and pick up his Camaro which was stored in our large garage, and leave his Jeep. However, this weekend was different. While Friday was a beautiful day, Saturday defied the weather forecasters and suddenly brought a horrendous storm. Evan and his fiancée, Gigi, were leaving his apartment, when a torrential downpour hit Worthington. His overpowered Camaro cannot handle any snow, and even rain can be a problem with his semi-slick tires. Evan and Gigi started to enter the on ramp to I-270. Even going just twenty miles per hour, Evan could not get the Camaro under control. He was sliding down the on-ramp into oncoming traffic. As he was entering the highway, the cars behind him and in the next lane either chose not to slow down or simply couldn't in the heavy rain. A semi clipped Evan's rear end and spun the car around into the right berm. The whole rear and of his car, from the axle back, was gone.

Pat and I were home, doing our normal Saturday chores around the house, when we got the call from Evan in late June 2009. We heard the magic words, "We are fine, but my car is totaled." The, "We are fine," part was great, but it was very scary when we realized what could have happened.

We quickly drove the eight miles to the crash site and met Gigi's parents there. There were lots of tears of joy and sadness.

Surprisingly, Evan and Gigi were totally unhurt—no injuries, no scratches, not even a stiff neck or sore back. The roll cage had saved them. It appears someone was looking out for them or gave Evan a hint to buy a roll cage if his hobby was going to be dangerous.

His car was a mess, with parts laying along the right berm for one hundred yards. It was not important at the time, but the racing parts and engine were unharmed.

The car was totaled, and we used the insurance money to salvage the engine and other key parts and put them in an almost identical used Camaro we bought. As is the thinking of a twenty-five-year-old, once you have the car in the shop, why not jack up the horsepower even further, to its current level of six hundred forty!

Bad Luck Part 3—Pat's Mom

The third bad-luck item came fairly quickly. Pat's mom, Gloria, had suffered a devastating stoke about seven years ago, which affected her right side. She could walk a little with a cane, but her right arm was useless, and she could not talk anymore. She could answer questions with a yes or no, and put two or three words together, but that was all. Her mind was still good though, and she still remembered well and still understood what you were saying. For any distance beyond about twenty feet, Gloria was moved around in a wheelchair by her husband, Fred.

On Friday morning, July 17, 2009, Fred and Gloria were staying at Pat's brother's house, across town from us. Gloria was walking out of the bathroom, and Fred was holding the wheelchair for her to sit in. They had done this maneuver thousands of times with no problem, but this time, Gloria fell forward instead of sitting down. By bad luck, they were close to the steps going upstairs, and Gloria hit her head on the first step. The damage was probably done by then. Fred, along with his son, Buddy, and daughter-in-law, Mary, got her up, and Gloria seemed fine. She didn't want to go to the hospital, so they sat her on the couch, and she appeared normal and watched TV for the next six hours.

Suddenly, about 3 p.m., Gloria started screaming and holding her head. They called the rescue squad, who quickly took her to the closest hospital. By the time she arrived, Gloria was already in a coma. She had a severe brain hemorrhage, and her skull was filling with blood, putting a lot a pressure on her brain. The net result was Gloria died two days later, being the last of three bad things in a month. While certainly very sad, Gloria had probably suffered enough with the aftereffects of the stoke. God may have decided it was her time.

13. Hernia

If God is looking out for you, you get a hernia! This is an odd statement; who would ever want a hernia? A hernia is better than the alternative. In the course of a lifetime, people do foolish things and lift too much weight or attempt activities they should know not to do. If you strain yourself to lift an object too heavy for you, either your back gives out or you get a hernia. Many people have back problems, and that is a terrible affliction. It is much better to tear out a hernia.

I was born with a birth defect and was prone to hernias. Almost immediately as a baby, when my mother was changing my diaper, she noticed I had a large bulge in my groin. Unfortunately, the large bulge was not my penis but next to my private parts! My pediatrician said I had a hernia on the right side, but he hoped it would not strangulate, as he wanted to wait until I was at least a year old to have it fixed. Well, I wasn't that cooperative. One night when Grandpa Ely was watching me while Mom and Dad were at Lake Park Pavilion for a dance, I started vomiting uncontrollably. This symptom is the sign of a strangulated hernia. Mom and Dad came home immediately, and I was rushed into emergency surgery at six months old. Everything worked out fine. I just have a large white scar on my right groin. For a few years after the surgery, as a little boy, I had "white coat syndrome" and screamed every time a nurse or doctor got near me. I think my wife still has that problem.

At every physical I have had since the surgery, the doctors always have me cough many times, because they are checking each side of my groin for hernias. They always say both sides are weak.

In was about 1985, and Pat and I were in our first house. Pat wanted to build a raised garden and landscape an area in the backyard. We had some landscape timbers delivered to our driveway. I needed to carry those around to the back and start leveling the ground and putting them into place. Thinking I was Hercules and not wanting to make too many trips, I put my arms around a bunch of timbers and carried them around to the back. I was able to do this in just a few trips and get started.

Well, I paid for that activity the next day and for the next several months. I noticed my left groin did not feel right and hurt. Since I was very familiar with the hernia test, I did it on myself, and whoops, I felt a bulge when I coughed. I finished the yard project, and it looked great with several levels, small pine trees, shrubs, and flowers. I went to my doctor and then a surgeon, and I had my hernia repaired a few months later. Evan was only about one year and a few months old, and I was not allowed to even lift him for a few weeks after surgery.

My surgeon gave me the Canadian hernia operation. After surgery, I was told to lift no more than a few pounds the first week, ten pounds the second week, twenty pounds the third week, thirty pounds the fourth week, forty pounds the fifth week, and fifty pounds after the sixth week. When I went back for my checkup, I did not see the surgeon but a rather attractive lady resident. It was a little tricky when she wanted to check my hernia, but I tried to breathe deeply and not think about what she was doing for fear of an embarrassing erection.

She told me to not be too macho again and suggested I not lift more than seventy-five pounds regularly. She said, "If you tear it again, the tissue will shred and be hard to fix." I lift weights, but don't lift anything heavier than seventy-five pounds from the floor. I try to be careful lifting items around the house.

In the Canadian hernia operation, as it was done in 1985, they want you awake so you can cough as they sew up each layer of muscle. So, rather than general anesthesia, you get a spinal. I don't mind general anesthesia but didn't really like the spinal. During surgery, I was somewhat awake. as they gave me a Valium IV to calm me down. Since I was awake and had heard of surgery horror stories, I reminded them of what side the repair was on, and I said, "Don't cut off anything important."

The resident joked, "We will just sew it back on if we do."

I could feel them cutting and pulling my insides during the surgery. I even jumped with pain a few times, and they had to increase the Valium IV to mitigate the pain. They had me cough three or four times at various stages, and they did a nice job. My repair is strong, and my scar is almost invisible.

Suitcase Back Injury

If you lift a heavy weight slowly and it is too much for your body, you may get a hernia. However, if you quickly make the wrong move with even a light weight, your hernia will not tear out. But you may hurt your back, as I did.

I had just returned from a long business trip, which involved several connecting flights. Weather delays left me about six hours late in getting home. I finally got home at 1 a.m., totally exhausted and really irritated. However, this was not a really good excuse to do something impulsive and reckless. Rarely is there a good excuse for this type of behavior. A five-second mistake can cost you hours or days of wasted time and effort. A really bad mistake can cost you more dearly in a lot of pain and suffering or considerable money.

After I pulled into the garage, I opened the trunk and yanked my suitcase out of the trunk with my left arm. Who knows why I used my left arm, as I am very right-handed. Pat was already upstairs in bed when I came in the house. After bending over to set down my suitcase in the den, I could not straighten up. I was stuck at a ninety-degree angle. When I tried to straighten up, a shooting pain went through my lower back. I have had other types of pain before that you could fight your way through, but this pain seemed to neutralize your muscles and stop them from working.

Back pain is really scary. Immediately, I understood the horrors stories I had heard over the years of friends' back problems. Now, I was bent over and suddenly felt broken, wondering if I would be able to straighten up again. Then, I waddled out of the den and down the hall to the staircase leading upstairs to our bedroom. Still bent over, I could climb one stair at a time using the handrail. Pat was asleep, and I did not want to disturb her or expose my stupidity. I was really exhausted now, and I crawled in bed and lay on my side, hoping for a better day tomorrow.

Pat and I called around to several chiropractors and found one who could take me on a Saturday morning. After some X-rays revealed no real damage, the chiropractor did a series of adjustments that started me back to normal. I was never so grateful for this miracle worker. God can only do so much to protect you from doing brainless things. Maybe he even lets you do them in the hope you learn something. Each of us should heed God's attempts at teaching us common sense, and we should pray for good judgment.

I learned that back trouble is awful, and you should try to avoid it at all costs. After several weeks of treatment, I was almost as good as new. But you will never be as good as new. A back problem can come back at any time. As long I do my back stretches, do sit-ups to keep my abs strong, maintain good posture, keep my weight under control, and avoid doing something dense, I am fine. It has been over eleven years, and I still can feel the tightness in that part of my back. And my problem was very minor compared to most back injuries! I was very good for about the last seven years but have since had a flare-up. I find it helps to see the chiropractor every three months.

14. Vietnam and the Draft

I graduated from Coshocton High School in 1969, at the height of the Vietnam War. The draft was still in effect, so any kid smart enough to get into college got the college deferment from military service. Male students studied hard then, because if you flunked out of college, you were drafted and sent to Vietnam. It was great motivation for kids to study and not goof off or party. Unfortunately, the college deferment had the effect that many draftees were poor and black, because they either did not qualify for college or could not afford to go to school.

If you were drafted, another way to avoid combat was to qualify for a military band. I saw a number of my high school band members frantically practicing and trying out for military bands. It was safer to play for a special government function in Washington, DC than be on guard in the jungles of Vietnam! The military bands are extremely good, however, so very few actually qualified.

Besides the college deferment I qualified for, I was not likely to get drafted for several reasons. Due to my hernia, I probably would have flunked the physical. Also, in about 1971, the government instituted a lottery, where each birthday was given a random number, and people were selected by that number. If, for example, May 1 drew number one, draft-eligible men born May 1 went first. By luck or the grace of God, my February 2 birthday was drawn 354th. In most years, they never took more than the first 150 numbers to get the men they needed, so I was pretty safe. As an additional measure of protection, my mom's uncle, Fred Launtenslager, was on the local draft board and could give special deferments for circumstances like being an only child. It seemed that God did not want me to see military action.

As it turns out, when you graduate from college, your college deferment ends, and you are now eligible for the draft. This is certainly fair but surprised most of us. Going on to graduate school, and I believe law school, dental school, medical school, or optometry, did not protect you, since these were not eligible for deferment.

I was going on to graduate school in chemistry, and I had heard of students being drafted and serving for several years before they could continue their graduate studies. To avoid this interruption and the danger, I made myself eligible for the draft the last week of 1972, my senior year at Wooster. I changed my status from 4-F to 1-A. Since my number was 354, and they were only up to about 120, I knew I was safe. Once you are passed over, you go to the bottom of the list and likely will never be called to serve.

In graduate school at Ohio State, I met Lowell, who had started his PhD in chemistry. After a year, he was drafted and spent two years in Vietnam and then came back to compete his degree. When he landed in Saigon, the local commander addressed the new troops and said he needed a new company clerk. Since Lowell was the most educated, the commander asked, "Soldier, you have a lot of education, so I suppose you can type?"

Lowell smartly said, "Certainly, sir, I can type." The commander then made Lowell company clerk, who would stay at the base and do paperwork, while everyone else he landed with would be going into the jungle for dangerous missions.

Lowell couldn't type at all, but he figured he would work hard and avoid getting shot. He was clever enough to protect himself. Had I been in the same situation, I would have stood there "like a wart on a pickle," as my father would say, and not uttered a sound. Then, I would be the one in the jungle dodging bullets.

Lowell said it was also a good job, because he compiled the venereal disease lists of which local hookers to avoid in town. That way, he could enjoy himself and avoid the rampant gonorrhea outbreak over there.

Lowell could take care of himself. Maybe God had to protect me, because I'm not street smart or too clever.

I love America and should have protected my country, but I would not have made a good soldier. I was a terrible Boy Scout and hated the camping, hiking, and wilderness stuff. In particular, a nice warm place to go to the bathroom is important to me. In retrospect, however, the experience would have made me grow up faster and been very good for me—assuming I survived.

15. Baseball

Baseball is a great game. God gave us brains to invent tools, machines, medicines, agriculture, and even recreational activities. Sometime in the late 1800s, we used our intelligence to invent a game where you hit a ball with a stick and then try to catch the ball. I think the games we invent are for our and his amusement.

While I didn't have much athletic talent, baseball was my best sport, and I played organized baseball for several years. Even though I loved baseball, I reached my limit in Little League. I could field and throw, but just could not see the fast pitches to hit well. In graduate school, I enjoyed a few years of slow-pitch softball, but that is not quite the same as real baseball.

One of the great privileges of being a parent is watching your children participate in different activities. My wife and I were blessed to watch Evan play baseball for eleven years. Athletically, he started by playing three years of soccer at age seven, but didn't really like it much. Even though he was only mediocre in soccer skills, by age nine, he was the fastest runner on his team and usually the fastest on the field. This surprised all of us, as neither Pat nor I would be considered fast runners. At least Evan could run up and down the soccer field and catch up with the ball even if he couldn't score.

I introduced Evan to baseball at a very early age. He and I would always play catch in the backyard, and he would bat with a Wiffle bat, since he was very little. Later, he moved on the hard balls and real bats.

By the time he started to play "Bronco Minor" Little League baseball at age ten, he already had some skills. He continued to play through three years of college at Otterbein College. In any competitive activity, the child and his parents learn some of life's lessons. People have different talent levels, people have different levels of interest and desire, some people are more competitive than others, some people will do anything to win, some people are quitters, and some people will argue for their team regardless of the situation or call. Even in sports, there can be a lot of politics and favoritism, and most sports are dangerous, and you can get hurt.

Evan always played in the recreation leagues, or the "rec" leagues, as they are called, as opposed to the "travel" teams or "select" teams. This was mostly because the rec leagues seemed to be the convenient, and I was an uneducated parent and did not know much about the travel teams. Travel teams in baseball, soccer, hockey, and so on, were the better teams, composed of better players who traveled around the state to play other travel, or "elite," teams. Rec leagues typically played fifteen games at local fields, only a few minutes' drive from most people's homes. In rec league baseball, each team has about fifteen players, and everyone—regardless of their skill level—gets to play at least half the game. The goal is fun, although each team is trying hard to win. The cost in rec leagues is minimal.

Travel teams are another matter. Each baseball team only has twelve players, and only the best will play. If you are the twelfth player and everyone shows up for all the games, you may not see much action. They typically play fifty games, and the cost may be $1,000 per year.

Pat and I did not know anything about the "system," so for several years, we didn't even know about the travel teams. Eventually, Evan did try out for the local travel team for two years. Since I had not played high school baseball, I did not know all the rules and nuances of the game, so Evan did not know all the terms the tryout coaches asked him. He hit and fielded pretty well, but he was outclassed. Evan was normal size, or maybe a little small for his age, and the other kids at the tryouts were gorillas. The better kids were huge for their age, as their testosterone must have kicked in early. I remember Evan getting about fifteen pitches and hitting about six nice singles in tryout batting practice. He was followed by Brad, who later played quarterback for a major college and eventually pro football. I believe they threw Brad five pitches, and he hit three home runs. That was all they needed to see. Brad was in, and Evan was put on the discard pile.

This rejection was not a big deal to Evan or us, because the other kids were obviously bigger and stronger, and travel baseball is a huge commitment. The number of games is ridiculous, and they travel all over the state, taking up most weekends.

Politically, however, in most communities, if your child does not play on a travel team in their chosen sport in middle school, they will never get on their high school team. They may not develop the skill level they need, and more important, they have no name recognition.

Evan played in the Dublin rec league from ages ten to sixteen, up though Pony League. When he was seventeen, there was no Senior Pony League, as our community did not have enough kids that age still playing. Most of the kids who still played were on travel teams. However, Evan could not break through to that league, because he had been out of the system too long. However, I did organize a "travel" team that played in the United States Specialty Sports Association system. Our team was made up of local kids who had played both rec and travel baseball and some who specialized in other sports, like track or soccer. We played against high school junior varsity teams around Columbus. We were outgunned on baseball knowledge and skill, but we managed to get four wins against fifteen losses. The fact that we won any games was an embarrassment to the junior varsity high school teams. In a few games we lost, we had a lead most of the game. Then suddenly, late in the game, an "error parade" would show up, and we would give up a bunch of runs and lose.

In both rec and travel teams, players' parents are usually the coaches. Not knowing the fine details of baseball, I was not qualified to be a head coach. However, I always volunteered to be an assistant coach, because they needed parents to help, and I was going to be at all the games anyway. Eventually, I was forced into being the head coach for the last three years of Evan's summer high school years, because their regular head coach was permanently kicked out of the league for arguing with the umpires. Parents' behavior at games on controversial plays was sometimes horrible and did not set a good example of sportsmanship for the players. As a coach, I never got mad at the umpires or even my own players, but as a father, I would get mad at Evan when he would make the rare error or mental mistake. I couldn't control this.

Our local rec league had tough rules on behavior. If a parent was being belligerent, the umpire could stop the game and tell the parent they had five minutes to leave the area. If the parent did not leave, the team would forfeit the game. In all cases, the parent eventually left, as the other parents would force them to walk away. Sometimes, this situation was a little tense, because a fifteen-year-old umpire was throwing out a forty-five-year-old man who was mad as hell. The umpires where not paid much to take the abuse they got. However, since umpires were the scarcest commodity (there were plenty of players and parents), they were given the most power.

Evan loved baseball and tried out for the school teams that played each spring. Unfortunately, due to his small size, the stiff competition, and some politics, he was cut from seventh, eighth, and freshman teams. Coaches knew who the "travel kids" were, looked at them seriously, and tended to ignore the rec league players. The problem for all coaches in almost any sport is they have a handful of great players who are easy to identify, but they also have about twenty kids who are decent and almost identical in ability. They have to pick another ten players, and let the others go.

Each year he was cut, it was a very devastating experience. He was heartbroken. Times like that are tough for parents. It is easy to watch your child succeed at an activity but difficult to watch them fail. You don't know what to do or how to console your child.

Some kids gave up baseball entirely, but Evan was determined and loved baseball, so he kept playing in summer leagues, trying to get bigger and better. He is probably about the only kid who played college baseball that never played on his high school team.

When he stopped playing after three years in college, I missed it more than he did.

What does baseball have to do with God? One of God's great gifts are memories. The key is to keep the good ones and delete the bad ones. I have Evan's ten most memorable baseball plays ingrained in my brain. Let me indulge myself and describe a few of his great plays. Then, you can remember the great moments for your children and friends in whatever activity they enjoyed:

- *Game-ending fly ball*—It was his first year in Little League, and Evan was playing center field. We had a one-run lead in the bottom of the last inning, and there were runners on first and second. A long, fly ball was hit to center field. Simultaneously, The coach and my wife loudly yelled, "Oh no!" With kids this young, almost no one catches a fly ball, because they don't have the spatial judgment at this age. And even if they get to the ball, it would usually hit their glove and bounce off onto the ground. Out of hundreds of fly balls that summer, I think I only saw four caught, and three were by Evan. He and I had practiced fly balls in the backyard for hours, so he was well prepared. On this play, everyone on the field—except, I believe, Evan—realized that if he caught the ball, we would win. If he dropped it, two runs would score, and we would lose. So, the ball went up, and I could see Evan looking directly at it. He slowly backed up about ten feet and easily caught it. Evan ran in from the outfield, all happy and relaxed, as I'm sure he didn't know how important that catch was.

- *Eight outs pitching*—In his second year of Little League (Bronco Major), the coach's plan was to take his three best players and rotate them between pitcher, catcher, and shortstop, figuring that would make the best of the talent he had available. Evan was one of the top three but had never pitched before. We had done a lot of throwing in the backyard but no actual preparation for pitching. In this league, throwing strikes was important, because there tended to be lots of walks. At that age, each team was limited to three walks per inning. Then, the pitchers was given as many pitches as needed to get the batter to strike out, get put out on a hit, or get a hit. Many innings started off with three walks to load the bases and then if an actual hit occurred, many runs scored. So, Evan pitched for three innings his first time. He struck out six, had two balls hit back to him on the mound and he threw out the batter at first, and one ball was hit to shortstop, who threw out the runner. Since he accounted for eight of the nine outs on his first try as pitcher, the couch was very impressed. That episode started his career as a pitcher, which he eventually preferred.

- *Three plays at shortstop*—In his third year in Little League (Junior Pony), Evan and his team were coached by two college baseball players, and Evan learned a lot. The coaches tended to keep the same kids in the same positions, so the biggest, strongest kid usually pitched, and Evan played shortstop. Again, each team had a mixture of good, fair, and poor players, but the goal was to play and have fun, and win if you could. During one particular game, the first batter hit the ball to short, and Evan threw him out. The second batter hit a fly to right field, and as was still somewhat typical, it hit the kid's glove, and he dropped it to put a runner on first. The third batter hit one to short, and Evan threw him out at first, while the runner at first moved to second. The fourth batter hit a fly to center, and the runner expected it to be caught, so he didn't move from second. The fielder dropped the ball, and now there were runners at first and second. The fifth batter flied to right, and again, the fielder dropped the ball, loading the bases as the runners on first and second moved up a base. Fortunately, the sixth batter hit the ball to short, and Evan threw him out. No runs scored, and Evan made all three outs. He came in and said, "I can't play all the positions." He was starting to feel the frustration of uneven talent on the rec league.

- *Struck out the side to win the league*—Evan finished his sophomore year in high school and was in his last year of Pony League. I was now the coach, because the other coach had been kicked out of the league. We were having a great season and were undefeated at 13–0. This had nothing to do with my coaching. I just set up the lineup and let the kids play without giving them much guidance during the game. We were playing our last game before the tournament was to start, and we wanted to finish undefeated. Of course, we were playing the other best team in the league. We were winning by a run, and the other coach's son came up to bat. Evan called a time out and came over to talk to me. He said, "I can't get this guy out. Let's walk him."

I asked, "Are you sure?

He said, "Last time we played him, he hit two doubles off of me, and two innings ago, he hit another double. Let's walk him."

 I said, "But that will load the bases."

"Dad, I'll strike the rest of these guys out. No problem."

I said, "Go ahead." Well, I was privileged to watch a miracle. He gave the other coach's son an intentional walk, which infuriated the coach. Then, Evan threw nine pitches as hard as he could to strike out the next three batters, and we finished the regular season undefeated.

- *Took one off the shin*—Evan had just completed his sophomore year at Otterbein College where he made the baseball team and was playing on their summer team. This was a wood bat league, so it was more true baseball then the regular season, where metal bats were used. Games were won by good pitching, good hitting, base running, and good fielding. Many regular college games are just home run contests, particularly as you get into the NCAA tournaments. In a wood bat league, Evan shined, as his control allowed him to work the hitter. An occasional bad pitch was a double and not a home run, unless the batter really had a good stroke and was strong. That summer, Evan had four wins and no losses, with a 1.0 ERA. They were playing the Athletics, which was a tough team Otterbein could not beat. Evan cruised along through six innings, only giving up a few hits and no runs. Otterbein had a seven-run lead in the seventh inning, when Evan threw a bad pitch, and the batter hit it right back to him. In most situations, when the ball was hit back to him, he would take a stab at it with his glove, mostly trying to protect himself. He would either catch it or knock it down and throw out the runner. But not this time. The ball was crushed, and Evan was knocked right off the mound. It hit his shin, which swelled up like a baseball; he was lucky his leg was not broken. He swears to this day that he can still feel the thread marks the baseball left on his shin. Both teams crowded around him to see if he was all right, and the coach motioned for a relief pitcher to come in and finish the game. Evan quickly stood up and hopped around on his good leg, saying, "It's my game, and I'm going to finish it." After a few minutes of Evan hoppling around and the coach talking to the ump, the coach let him continue. Evan gave up a few hits and two runs, but finished the game. Double-header games were only seven innings, so he could finish that game.

- *Nine-inning complete game*—The same summer of the "shin ball," Evan started a nine-inning game against Capital University's summer team. Pat and I went to every game, but this time, Gigi's parents came, and my cousin Craig and his wife were there to watch Evan. He pitched great. We all yelled after Evan retired each batter. Between innings, one of Evan's teammates in the dugout asked, "What's going on? I didn't know we were playing in the World Series." Evan pitched the entire nine innings, which he had never done before. At one point, he was getting tired and let out a groan as his threw his fastball as hard as he could, similar to the way some tennis players groan during maximum effort. A few pitches later, Evan groaned loudly on a slow change-up, making the batter swing early, thinking he was getting a fastball. We all got a good laugh at that player's expense.

As a pitcher, Evan did not throw hard and relied on accuracy and his curveball. Pat used to get really nervous when his pitched, as the whole team was depending on him, and she didn't want her "little boy" to do poorly and feel bad. I used to get nervous, but after a few games, I realized he had things under control.

You could tell early if it was going to be good day or a bad day. Evan would usually throw a number of curveballs in the first inning. If Evan could control his curveball, keep it low in the strike zone, and the umpire would give Evan the low strikes, I knew it would be a great day. If Evan couldn't control his curve and the umpire had a small strike zone, it was going to be a long day. Then, all you could hope for was some good hitting and fielding by his teammates. Evan tended to get great fielding by his teammates. Maybe they knew his pitches were going to get hit, so they needed to pay attention. Evan was always very appreciative of his teammates, acknowledging them for good plays. He liked his teammates a lot, and he knew if he thanked them, they would be diving on the ground to stop the next hit from getting through.

Notice that none of my favorite memories are about Evans hitting. He never stressed hitting that much. In almost every league at every age, he batted over .300, and he had lots of key hits. But I don't remember many of those. Evan preferred to hit the ball to the opposite field, which was left for him, and run like wild to beat out the throw, even if the third baseman picked it up. He never swung hard to try to get a home run. Even when he got a lot bigger and stronger, he preferred to swing easy and bat for average.

If I had been really lucky, my son would have had a ninety-mile-per-hour fastball, but in college he topped out at eighty-three to eighty-four, which will not get you into the pros. From a very early age, Evan was ambidextrous. At about age one, he and I would sit on the floor and toss a little rubber ball back and forth. He could throw it to me with either hand and didn't show a preference. Whatever hand he caught it, with he would throw it back to me. If I thought about it, I could toss it back to him with my left hand, but it was a weak toss. I am the opposite of ambidextrous.

When eating, his preference was to use the spoon in his left hand. Pat wanted him to be right-handed, so she would keep switching the spoon back to his right hand. He eventually kept it there. Pat really wanted him to write with his right hand, so that was her motivation. When playing sports, Evan would throw with his right hand but preferred to bat left-handed. This is actually a pretty good combination for baseball. He plays golf right-handed, because it is easier to get clubs and good instruction. Also, he didn't want to confuse the baseball swing with the golf swing.

However, we should have let him learn to throw with his left hand. In professional baseball, a right-handed pitcher needs to throw ninety-three miles per hour to get noticed. However, a left-hander can get the attention of scouts at about eighty-four miles per hour. Regardless, God gave us the thrill of watching him play a sport he loved for eleven years.

16. Golf—God Has a Sense of Humor

Golf is one of the greatest inventions of mankind. It is an elegant yet insane game. I believe the invention of golf shows that God has a sense of humor. It is such a ridiculous game, God has to be laughing at the stuff that happens on a golf course.

I love to play golf; I just love to play it. I'm not very good, being mostly a bogey golfer with a 20 handicap. Golf is my second-most favorite activity after sex and just before playing the trumpet. Actually, my most favorite activity is watching my son do something. I would always give up any of the top three if he had a baseball game, music concert, or bodybuilding contest. Now, on Sundays, he and I usually play golf, which is great. Since he is an adult now, and an accountant, watching him do accounting is not on the list of activities I care to see.

Golf is a totally unusual sport in that it involves skill and a lot of luck. It is one of the few sports where, for a few seconds, an amateur can be just as good as the best pros. You can play terrible all day and then suddenly hit a seven-iron two feet from the hole. It is these great shots that make golf so addictive. You remember the one or two great shots you had in a round of golf and forget the other sixty shots that were decent and the thirty that were really lousy.

There is nothing on a baseball field that can match that. No matter how much I play, I am not suddenly going to hit a four hundred-foot home run. If I played third base, there is no play I could make that would work like the pros. Most balls would be hit at me so hard, I would either not see them, could not field them, or would get injured trying to field them. If the ball was hit slow enough I could catch it, I could not throw out the runner going to first. The distance is too far, and my arm is too old.

But in golf, momentary glory is a regular event. At any skill level, a person can make a thirty-foot putt or chip one in from off the green. It may happen once a week or once a year, but most golfers get that joy of brief perfection. The following are examples of fortuitous events on a golf course that shows me God has a sense of humor.

Broke Forty

I've only broken forty for nine holes about ten times in my life. The first time was an illustration of God's humor. I was playing with three good friends from our Monday night league: Clancy, Dave, and Terry. We were playing eighteen, and my first nine was poor: and I shot fifty-two. We grabbed a quick snack and went on the play the back nine. Suddenly, my every shot was great, and I made every putt. I followed my front nine fifty-two with a one over par thirty-seven on the back. I didn't change anything in my swing that I knew of; suddenly I was just good. Nobody shoots fifty-two and thirty-seven; that's ridiculous. Dave, who is an excellent golfer and normally would shoot thirty-eight and thirty-eight for a seventy-six couldn't believe what he was seeing. If I needed a twelve-foot putt for a par, it just rolled into the hole. I went from a disaster to beating him on the back nine. It was all Dave could do not to throw up. When someone shoots fifty-two and thirty-seven, God has to be laughing.

Under Par

It was 1982, and I was in the company Monday night golf league. I was younger then and a somewhat better golfer, but still mostly a bogey golfer. I was used to the occasionally great shot, but on this Monday, everything came together. My driving was long and straight, my irons and chipping were great, and my putting was fantastic. I only hit one bad shot in those nine holes, and I followed that with a chip four feet from the hole. I made every put I needed, whether from three or ten feet. That day, I shot a one *under par* thirty-five for nine holes. My normal score would have been about forty-five.

Hole in One

Many nights in the summer, I play nine holes of golf by myself just before dark. It is cooler then and a nice relaxing time to play. I always figured if I ever got a hole in one, it would be playing by myself with no witnesses, so no one would believe me. Well, one Saturday morning, I was playing with two friends—Jeff and Rick—and as usual, was not playing very well. I just could not do much of anything: drive, irons, chip, or putt. We came to the seventh hole, which is a one hundred sixty-yard par three. Suddenly, out of nowhere, I hit a perfect 5 iron, which hit twenty feet in front of the hole and rolled right in. It was unbelievable, and I had two witnesses.

Long Drive

Evan was about twelve and we were playing the thirteenth hole on a Sunday, when I sliced a drive way right. It hit the cart path and bounced forward and left. Then it hit the cart path again, and again, and again. The cart path was tilted slightly left and went along the right side of the hole. It all it bounced about nine or ten times before it finally stopped in the rough, well beyond the far traps. To our best calculation, my drive went three hundred thiry yards! Considering my best drives at that time went about two hundred fifty yards, this was a real gift. God had to be laughing!

Bounce onto the Green

On one particular Wednesday, our company president was fired for unscrupulous activity. On Thursday, our purchasing manager had scheduled a golf outing with one of our suppliers at the prestigious Firestone Country Club. Since our president was gone, the purchasing manager was desperate to find a replacement, and he picked me. The course was too hard for me in general, but I survived. In typical fashion I sliced an iron badly to the right on hole eight, and it hit off the edge of the cart path and bounced directly left onto the green at Firestone, eight feet from the hole. I got an easy par totally due to luck.

Member Bounce

In golf, there is what is known as the "member bounce." If you play a course often enough, the course seems to give you fortuitous bounces out of trouble into a more playable area. Errant shots can bounce off trees into the middle of the fairway. It was Sunday, about five years ago, on hole twelve. I sliced my drive right for the creek. My ball hit off a flat stone near the creek and bounced forward about fifty yards. The net result was I had a two hundred ninety-yard drive and was sitting near the green. Every time my son observes one of my "member bounces," he is appalled at my luck of hitting terrible shots and ending up in decent locations.

He has had a few of these. Being twenty-six years old with some talent, he is a much better golfer than I am and has an 8 handicap. A few years ago, he was playing well and on his was to breaking eighty and getting an even par thirty-six on the back nine. All day, his shots had been very good, and on the back nine, he had been perfect. It was the last hole, which is hard. Your second shot needs to go over the water if you want to get to the par four in two. Suddenly, he pulled his second shot way left, about thirty yards off target, into a big, weeping willow tree. By all rights, his ball should have hit the tree and dropped in the water, or hit the tree and bounced right into the thick rough behind some other trees. Instead, his ball hit a tree branch, bounced way up into the air, slightly right, and landed softly on the green, about ten feet from the hole. He two putts for the par and says he deserves that after watching all my lucky bounces.

Mowing Grass

Like most homeowners, I have mowed a lot of grass. For many years, I pushed the mower. Then, with encouragement from my wife, we bought a small riding mower. We soon discovered that Pat loves to mow grass. She loves to mow grass as much as I love to play golf. Pat really likes plants, whether they be grass, flowers, or vegetables. She loves to take care of them. Combine her love for grass with her perfectionist nature, and you can see why she likes a perfect lawn—green, no weeds, perfectly cut and edged. She finds riding a lawn mower to be very relaxing. A few years ago, on our wedding anniversary, I bought her a big, new, riding mower! She was ecstatic. That was just not normal behavior. A number of times in the summer, I will be heading off to play a round of golf just as Pat is pulling the mower out of the garage to cut the lawn. Having a wife who loves to move grass and encourages me to play golf is truly a blessing from God.

Much of golf is dumb luck, but I still believe God looks down and laughs at our futility at this silly game. However, he is probably not thrilled with the language emitted by most of us golfers, as shots go into the wrong places. I have tried to observe the third commandment and not take the Lord's name in vain as I struggle down the course. Other words do come out, however.

17. Gifts from God

I don't know whether it is luck or gifts from God, but most of us get some gifts to improve our life. I believe there are six main areas of gifts:

- Good parents
- Personal health
- Great life partner
- Children
- Interesting job or unique skill
- An appreciation for God

Why we all don't get all the gifts, I don't know. Hopefully, you have a number of these in your life. I've always thought I had more than my fair share of gifts.

Great Parents

The first great gift God gave me was fantastic parents. Mom had trouble getting pregnant, and I was a breech baby, so she had a lot of trouble giving birth to me. Both my parents naturally seemed to know what to do to raise a kid. They were not overly demonstrative people, but I knew they both loved me a great deal. They had rules, but were not overly strict disciplinarians. They were both very time conscious. Never ever be late. This stemmed from my mother's father being a lawyer, and he could just not be late to court.

As I said earlier, Dad was the last honest man, but that may be the subject of another book. Our family attended church every Sunday, and Mom and Dad worked on all the church committees. My father was strict on grades; his only requirement was all As!

Dad was not cheap, but he was thrifty by nature because of his upbringing. He did have one great philosophy: "I will buy you anything that *we can afford* that *you will use*." The key is, "you will use" it, not play with it once and discard or try it out and, in a few weeks, give it up. If I wanted a new toy as a little kid or a new trumpet as a high school student, I needed to convince him it was what I really wanted and it would get plenty of use.

Mom and Dad were great parents!

Health

The second gift is health. I've always been relatively healthy and felt good. My list of broken arms, sprained ankles, hernias, minor back trouble, a few kidney stones, psoriasis, and my neck trouble would seem to indicate otherwise. But these ailments are just part of life and only ruin a few days.

Wife and Children

My wife and our son have made my life full as described in the previous chapters.

Job and Skill

An interesting job or having a particular skill is another wonderful gift. In my sophomore year of high school, I took chemistry from Mr. McKissick. He was a great, old teacher and really loved chemistry. He was so old that he had also taught my mother, father, and Uncle Frank when they were in high school. Almost right away, I thought chemistry was really interesting and knew I wanted to do it for the rest of my life. After thirty-three years in the industry and forty-five years since my class with Mr. McKissick, I still find it interesting.

Lab work was always interesting to me, but after a few years in my job, I moved into research management and now am in sales and account management. I still do some paper chemistry in talking to our research and development folks about new products, and I still talk chemistry with our customers. I do miss lab work though and occasionally will formulate a cleaner on the weekends in our laundry room to test on something around our house. Managing people is not something I miss, however, after eighteen years of guiding people through projects, bugging them to write final reports, helping them through various marital troubles, helping them manage their finances, and telling them they are not going to get a big raise just because they spent too much, and so on. I did enough management. And really, I managed a truly great group of chemists and people. However, people just have different ways of working, and they have personal problems.

As my son got older, I would tell him that 20 percent of my job is really interesting and uses my PhD in chemistry. The other 80 percent is common sense, hard work, and just doing what needs to get done. If a person can mentally focus on the good part of their occupation and just do but ignore the boring part, they will enjoy their job, and their life will be better.

However, it still is a job, and that is why they have to pay you to do it. I love the saying, "The worst day I ever had playing golf is still better than the best day I had working." This isn't really true, but it's close.

Regarding skills, I wasn't given many, but I can do almost anything in a mediocre fashion. I'm decent at playing the trumpet and fair at golf, both of which I have worked at very hard. I can also swim, ballroom dance, bowl, play baseball, play tennis, and do archery with some combination of skill and ineptitude. Maybe God's gift is to let you enjoy various activities, even if your skill level is less than desirable.

Appreciation for God

The last gift is an appreciation for God and the inherent beauty in life. A general optimism and well-being of life is invaluable. I'm a "glass half full" person and try to see the bright side of things.

Maybe I'm lazy. Feeling down, depressed, or angry takes too much energy. I always prefer to be optimistic. I can be realistic but not gloomy. The snow out my back window is beautiful, not a travel problem. Although last winter, I did fall hard on my butt in the icy driveway!

By believing in God, I think I have an inner peace. I have learned that I need to go about my daily activities with hard work and good sense, and most things will work out. Between my family and God, I am not alone in struggling with the world.

Again, I've always thought I had more than my fair share of luck. This does not make much sense, as I am far from perfect. I am an only child and too self-centered. I'm too materialistic and concerned with money. I am a notorious girl watcher. While I would never cheat on my wife, I've been known to enjoy the sight of attractive women. And rarely do I go out of my way to help other people physically. I am introverted and just stick to myself—and try not to get involved. The one good thing I do regularly is donate blood. There always seems to be a shortage, and at least I can help out there every few months. If you are healthy and not too afraid of needles, I highly recommend donating.

So, why in the world would God protect me? Maybe because I believe; maybe I have a larger purpose. Who knows?

18. Why So Many Different Religions and Types of People

When I was in graduate school, I sometimes went to McDonald's for lunch. Many days I had the first Big Mac of the day right after they closed breakfast. On one day, I had gotten my meal and was struggling with the straw dispenser to get a straw for my drink. Just then, a little black boy, about three years old, handed me a straw. He was really cute and had a big afro, as was a common hairstyle in 1975. The expression on his face was so innocent, and he just wanted to help a stranger. I looked at him and thought how cute and pure he was. He did not know the bigotry and hate common in the real world. I wondered how long he would stay this innocent and why we all couldn't be that way. I took the straw, said, "Thank you," and started to leave with my lunch. By then, his mother saw what her son was doing, and I could see a little apprehension in her face, as she wondered why her boy was talking to a strange white man. But we nodded to each other and went our separate ways. For a second, she saw the innocence of the situation but was probably going to tell her son to stay away from strangers, because they can be dangerous. Every mother has to do that, and eventually we all lose our innocence.

The College of Wooster was founded by the Presbyterian Church in 1866. One of the graduation requirements was that everyone had to take a religion class. There were many from which to choose, but I chose comparative religion. It was an excellent course, except age nineteen is not the right time to study comparative religion. We would appreciate it more at age forty or older. The class compared Catholics to Protestants, Jews, Muslims, Hindus, Buddhists, and so on.

I've always wondered, *Why are there so many religions?* I was raised a Presbyterian, and my wife is a Catholic. Anglican, Baptist, Congregational, Lutheran, Methodist, Mennonite, Mormon, Nazarene, Pentecostal, Presbyterian, Quaker, Reformed, Salvation Army, and many smaller groups are all Protestants. Apparently there were lots of disagreements and "protesting" about different aspects of religion. Protestants, Catholics, and Greek Orthodox all are Christians. Christians, Jews, and Muslims all basically use the Old Testament. They all believe in one similar God and have many similar beliefs. Getting into the details, there are differences in beliefs and ceremonies, but to me, these are minor differences. Catholics have Communion at every service, but Presbyterians have it four to twelve times a year. The sacrament has a special meaning about the Last Supper and the "Body of Christ," but how often it is observed is not important to me. All these religions believe in a supreme being, who wants his people to believe in him and generally be good, kind, and nice people.

The Ten Commandments

The Old Testament gives us the Ten Commandments as the basis for proper behavior. Different versions and translations of the Bible have slightly different commandments, but they are essentially the same thoughts. While the Ten Commandments as such are not explicitly mentioned in the Muslim Qur'an they occur in various verses with virtually identical meanings.

1. I am the Lord thy God and thou shalt have no other gods before me.
2. Thou shalt not make any graven images.
3. Thou shalt not take the Lord's name in vain.
4. Honor the Sabbath.
5. Honor thy father and mother.

6. Thou shalt not kill.
7. Thou shalt not commit adultery.
8. Thou shalt not steal.
9. Thou shalt not bear false witness.
10. Thou shalt not covet.

Buddhism and Hinduism are less familiar to me and somewhat different, as they originated in India/Asia rather than in the Middle East. I hope Buddhists and Hindus are not offended if I misinterpreted their beliefs in my summaries of their religions below.

Buddhism

From Wikipedia and other sources, Buddhism is a religion and philosophy based on the teachings of Siddhartha Gautama, commonly known as the Buddha ("the awakened one"). Although Buddhism is mostly associated with China and the Asian countries, the Buddha lived and taught in northeastern India around the fifth century BC. After his Enlightenment, Buddha's first sermon centered on the Four Noble Truths. These truths are foundation of Buddhism:

- The truth of suffering
- The truth of the cause of suffering
- The truth of the end of suffering
- The truth of the path that frees us from suffering

The Truth of Suffering
The First Noble Truth often is translated as, "Life is suffering."

The Truth of the Cause of Suffering
The Second Noble Truth teaches that the cause of suffering is craving or thirst. We continually search for something beyond ourselves to make us happy. But no matter how successful we are, we are never really satisfied. The Buddha taught that this thirst grows from ignorance of ourselves. We strive for material possessions and status, searching for a sense of well-being. However, we grow frustrated when our lives don't live up to our expectations.

The Truth of the End of Suffering

The Buddha taught that through diligent practice, we can put an end to craving. The enlightened being exists in a state called Nirvana.

The Truth of the Path that Frees Us from Suffering

The Buddha reveals that the treatment for our "illness" is the Eightfold Path. Unlike many other religions, in Buddhism, there is no particular benefit to merely believing. Instead, the emphasis is on living the doctrine and walking the path. A Buddha is anyone who has realized the enlightenment that ends the cycle of birth and death and liberation from suffering.

The Fourth Noble Truth Is the Eightfold Path

The Eightfold Path is the means by which enlightenment may be realized:

1. Right View
2. Right Intention
3. Right Speech
4. Right Action
5. Right Livelihood
6. Right Effort
7. Right Mindfulness
8. Right Concentration

The Path is divided into three main sections: wisdom, ethical conduct, and mental discipline.

Wisdom: Right View and Right Intention are the wisdom path. Right View is about perceiving the true nature of ourselves and the world around us. Right Intention refers to the commitment one needs to be fully engaged in Buddhism.

Ethical Conduct: Right Speech, Right Action, and Right Livelihood are the ethical conduct path. Our speech, actions, and how we make a living should do no harm to others and cultivate wholesomeness in ourselves.

Mental Discipline: Through Right Effort, Right Mindfulness, and Right Concentration, we develop the mental discipline to avoid delusion of ourselves and others. Meditation is encouraged to focus the mind and give clarity to the world.

To me, the basic beliefs of Buddhism, particularly the Ethical Conduct section, are very similar to the Ten Commandments. In Buddism, a person should be a good, honest person who does no harm to other people. Buddhism does stress being a less-materialist person.

One problem I see with Buddhism is that many of man's great discoveries and inventions could not have been achieved without the "thirst" for knowledge or personal success. I think some "craving" or "hunger" is needed to keep us motivated each day, but I probably have not found enlightenment.

Hinduism

According to Wikipedia, Hinduism is the dominant religion of South Asia and was formed of diverse traditions with no single founder. Hinduism does not have a set system of beliefs. It covers many religious beliefs and, thus, is viewed as the most complex of all world religions. Hinduism is one of the largest faiths and is also the oldest, dating back to prehistory (5500–2600 BC).

Hinduism allows complete freedom of belief and worship. This tolerance to differences in belief makes it truly unique. Many Hindus believe that the goals of spiritual life can be attained through any religion, as long as it is practiced sincerely.

Hinduism does not have the concepts of heresy and blasphemy. To me, this is an important and special concept. Most religions, or at least most religious organizations, are paranoid of losing their followers and, more important, their financial backing, so they are not very tolerant of other religions or beliefs. Most religions would not appreciate or approve of their followers taking a course in comparative religion.

Many Hindus believe that the soul of every person is eternal and, therefore, believe in reincarnation. This cycle of birth, death, and rebirth allows people to enjoy the pleasures of a perishable body again and again. One theory is that after several reincarnations, a soul eventually seeks unity with the cosmic spirit.

The ultimate goal of life is union with God, attainment of mental peace, and elimination from worldly desires.

Concept of God
Hinduism's concept of God is complex and allows devotion to a single god while accepting the existence of others.

Objectives of Human Life
There are four objectives of human life:

- righteousness
- livelihood, wealth
- sensual pleasure
- liberation, freedom

You achieve these objectives by several Yogas

- the path of love and devotion
- the path of right action
- the path of meditation
- the path of wisdom

Traditionally, the life of a Hindu is divided into four phases:

1. *Student phase* is spent in celibate contemplation, increasing one's knowledge under the guidance of a guru.
2. *Householder phase* is when one marries and satisfies the physical pleasures of the body and financial pursuits in

professional life. The Hindu householder supports one's parents, children, guests, and holy figures.

3. *Retirement phase* is a gradual departure from the material world. During this phase, one transfer duties to one's children, spending more time in religious practices and embarking on holy pilgrimages.

4. *Detachment phase* involves renouncing all worldly attachments to find God through separation from worldly life and peacefully shedding the body.

Hindus practice nonviolence and have respect for all life, because divinity is believed to permeate all beings, including plants and animals. In accordance with the belief in nonviolence many Hindus practice vegetarianism to show respect for higher forms of life.

Some Hindus choose to live a monastic life in pursuit of liberation or another form of spiritual perfection. Monastics commit themselves to a life of simplicity, celibacy, detachment from worldly pursuits, and the contemplation of God.

Hinduism contrasts most other religions in that it recognizes the physical pleasures of sex and wealth, and these are stages in the lifecycle that are strived for. Most religions avoid the mention of sex or at least that it is enjoyable.

Parts of Buddhism and Hinduism are very similar, including the search for simplicity, purity, and nirvana. Again, these religions advocate truth, honesty, good behavior, and kindness to other people, not unlike the Ten Commandments.

Maybe God gave us these different religions, cultures, and ethnic groups as a test to see if we all can be basically good people and get along with each other. Unfortunately, we are definitely failing this test miserably.

The Ten Commandments are certainly a good starting list for our behavior and the basis for most countries' laws. If you can follow these ten rules, you have a fantastic chance at being a good person in this world.

Regarding the commandment against killing, are there any circumstances when killing is acceptable? What if a loved one, your family, or even a friend or stranger is being attacked? I think what God is telling us is that we should use any means short of killing someone to protect your family, *if at all possible.* In the end, a person has to protect one's family and country. So, avoiding killing may not be possible, but then we will have to answer to God.

19. Poverty, Disease, War, Natural Disasters

All of us have probably wondered, *If God is all powerful, why is there poverty, disease, war, and natural disasters?* This is an impossible question. Maybe God can only control so much. My belief is that again, this may be part of a test. Are we willing to help the less-fortunate, are we willing to work on cures for diseases, are we willing to get along? Again, we may not be doing well on this test.

Let's look at the animal world as a contrast. I believe the animal kingdom was created by God and modified by evolution. Being created by God, animals are not inherently bad or evil. However, they do live by survival of the fittest. The strong eat the weak and breed more. It is a very efficient system. Animals that are sick, elderly, injured, or born with defects are eaten by stronger, younger animals. There is no need for Social Security, Medicare, or other social programs. Once an animal is weak, it is gone.

There is a slogan used by some businesses: "Every morning a lion wakes up and knows that to eat and survive it must be able to outrun the slowest of the gazelles. Every morning a gazelle gets up and knows it must be able to outrun the fastest lion to survive. Therefore, when you get up in the morning, you better start running."

In reality, the gazelle does not need to be able to outrun the fastest lion, because it probably can't. An individual gazelle just needs to be able to outrun the slowest of the other gazelles, because those are the ones that will be eaten.

There is an old joke about two friends fishing at a lake. They are wearing boots and standing in a few feet of water, fishing, talking, and having a good time, when they notice a bear coming over a hill about half a mile away. Bob yells, "We better get to the truck," which is a long way away in the other direction, and he starts running wildly toward the truck struggling, to gain much speed in his clumsy boots. Bill gets out of the water and quickly changes from his boots to his tennis shoes, which were near the shore. Bill starts running toward the truck and eventually catches Bob, still floundering in his boots. Bob says, "The bear is gaining on us. I don't think you can outrun the bear, even in those shoes."

Bill answers, "I don't think I can outrun him either, but I don't have to. I just have to outrun you." The net result is survival of the fittest.

The animal kingdom has large numbers of vegetarians and a few predators to thin out the weak from the herds of the vegetarians. There are also scavengers that eat dead animals and basically clean up the garbage of the animal world. This is a very elegant and efficient system either devised by a superior being or evolved by trial and error—or both.

Mankind does not necessarily work by survival of the fittest. In a general sense, the fittest, strongest, smartest, most ingenious, or most cunning do survive and prosper, and maybe even breed more. Many of mankind's problems stem from not adhering to the survival of the fittest system. The elderly, weak, less intelligent, less healthy, deformed, or just plain lazy occupy much of society's resources and thinking. However, maybe that is the point. Man is above the animal kingdom, because he does not entirely work by survival of the fittest. Maybe one of man's jobs is to care for the weak and provide them a measure of care. This may be one of God's ultimate tests.

However, there must be some common sense in this system. If too many people are weak or lazy, the strong cannot help them. Society collapses, and we may end up with no laws or morality. Then, survival of the fittest takes over. I believe God wants us to care for the weak and figure out a way for society to survive the delicate balance of priorities and resources. I don't believe we as a society, and certainly not our government, are passing this test. Somehow, we have to give reasonable care for the unfortunate, but separate out and motivate the lazy and those who take advantage of the system.

Maybe our health-care system should be designed to prevent illness and cure reasonable diseases. Spending millions of dollars prolonging the life of a severely ill elderly person or a hopelessly deformed baby may not be the best use of our limited resources. These are incredibly difficult questions, with no easy answers.

If we truly believe in God, the good people go to heaven, so death should not be viewed no negatively. We should be less afraid to die, and we should fear the death of our relatives less.

Next time you turn on one of the animal shows, watch a predator chase. The prey runs hard to get away, changes directions, and climbs up obstacles trying to save itself. However, when the predator finally catches it by the throat, it seems to me you can see the prey give up and let the end happen. They seem to accept the inevitable better than people do.

When you watch the nightly news, you see all kinds of misfortune and calamities occur to people all over the globe. Every year, thousands of people are injured or killed in earthquakes, hurricanes, tornadoes, and floods. I wonder why people need to experience this much suffering, but the one thing that really puzzles me is why do tornadoes strike churches? Trailer parks have always been a magnet for tornadoes, but why do churches get hit? You would think God would protect them. Maybe he cannot control all these things. Maybe protecting a church would be unfair to the rest of the devastated areas. Maybe it is to test our faith.

20. Prayer

Prayer is part of almost every religion and is a very private matter. I pray every night, but I don't think even my wife knows that I do and when. I say a modified version of a simple prayer that my mother taught me years ago.

> God is good, God is great, and we thank you for our food. Thank you God for everything you have done for me today. Let Patti, Evan, and I have a long happy healthy life together. Above all, protect our son, Evan. Keep him safe and let him lead a good, happy, and useful life.

Then, there may be specific thanks or requests depending on recent events. As my mother's health declined, I added, "Let my mother be happy with her situation. Keep her mind and body functioning until the end. Don't let her slowly fall apart and get confused and end up in a nursing home. When the time is right, let the end come quickly and painlessly."

I believe you should keep your prayers fairly brief and not ask for too much. You should only ask for really important things.

We all have important questions about prayer:

- Do prayers work?
- Why do some prayers seem to be answered and others not?

I do believe some prayers work. God certainly has too many requests and problems to be able to deal with more than a few of them. If he answered all our prayers, there would be no logic to life. All diseases would be cured, no one would have money problems, no one would argue. If all our prayers were answered, man would have no purpose in life. Also, maybe God's powers are limited. Maybe by answering only a few, he is testing our faith.

I believe that if you have a terrible disease like cancer, prayer will not cure it. Prayer may extend your life, it may lesson your pain, it may help you and your family deal with the situation, but I don't think any amount of prayer is going to make the cancer go away.

Again, save your prayers for the most important topics. Don't cross your heart before you step to the plate in baseball, and certainly don't thank God after you hit the game-winning home run. I hope God has better things to worry about. To me, the only legitimate prayer prior to a sporting event is to ask that you not get injured or you not injure another player.

However, I believe it is important to pray, to admit to yourself and God what is really important to you. And God will answer some of your prayers!

21. Behavior and Family Arguments

Many of us attend church or religious services, where we pray and hear expositions about being better people. We are pious in church, thank God for our blessings, and promise to be kind, gentle, and thoughtful to other people. Why is it that as soon as the church door shuts behind us, we forget what just happened the last hour? Even in the church parking lot, we may cut off someone with our car in a mad rush to get to lunch or our next activity. Is this what the church service just taught us? Too often we are good people *in* church but rude, inconsiderate sinners everywhere else. It is probably easy to think of examples of "supposedly religious" people or regular "churchgoers" treating you badly. They may have insulted you, been overly harsh in a business deal, or even tried to cheat you. They may have not liked your driving and swore at you, or argued in an uncontrollable fashion at a sporting event in which both your children participated. Those examples of being treated badly are readily recalled. What about the times where you behaved in a non-Christian or nonreligious fashion?

I have seen numerous mother–daughter, father–daughter, father–son, mother–son, and brother–sister confrontations in families, and I thought, *Is that how Jesus would have wanted you to behave?* It takes two to argue, and neither "religious" person will back down or try to defuse the situation. Rather than say something calming, we tend to say something that infuriates the other person more. Why is that? We probably expected our family member to treat us much better, so we retaliate in kind. And forget religion; I am going to win this argument!

Being an only child, I hate confrontation and am not well equipped to hold my own in a quarrel. I had no brothers or sisters with which to compete and was always the center of attention, so family arguments are an unknown arena for me.

I have been privileged to watch several verbal masters handle disagreements in the business world. The following are three examples from business situations that you might find useful in personal or family confrontations. They keep the heated discussion from turning into a full-fledged argument or worse. Also, these techniques may help you get your points across and "win" the discussion.

Dave—Stay Calm

Dave was our company president and the smartest businessman I have met. He could quickly gather information, get to the root of a problem, and work out a course of action to move the business ahead. He was a master of the English language and could really handle himself in a group of people.

Dave's best technique in a confrontation was to stay calm. No matter how serious or emotionally charged a situation was, Dave kept his voice at the same level and did not get mad. This behavior gave him distinct advantages: he remained logical and could out-think his mad adversary. To others in the meeting, Dave always appeared in control and the person taking the higher ground. And by staying calm, he would further infuriate his opponent, who then got more irrational. Sometimes, however, Dave was mean and would even do this in fun. He would insult the other person or their department to get them off balance, and when they responded with an insult of their own, Dave would stay calm and not respond emotionally. He would wind them up 'til they almost exploded.

Several of us managers were in a small meeting in Dave's office, along with the Harold, the VP of manufacturing. Dave wanted some changes done and a plant manager fired, so he challenged Harold and insulted one of his plants. Within a few minutes, Harold was bright red in the face, and little drops of spit were shooting from his mouth as the responded to Dave comments and accusations. Dave was calm and kept pushing. I felt sorry for Harold, but at the same time was trying to hold back some laughter, as Dave was really playing him.

In the end, Dave was the division president, so he was going to win the argument anyway: we would do what he wanted. If Harold had been able to remain calm and respond to Dave's questions and accusations calmly, he would have been able to get his points across better, plus avoid skyrocketing blood pressure.

Dave would not always stay perfectly calm. He could get forceful to get his point across in a large meeting, but he always stayed professional and fairly calm.

Every week on Friday, Dave scheduled a lunch management team meeting with about fifteen of his top managers, including manufacturing managers who had to fly in for these two-hour meetings. Fortunately, he included me in these meetings, where I learned a lot and thought they were fun. Most people dreaded these meetings as the worst part of their workweek. They were scared that they or their department were going to get taken to task. R&D is mostly future oriented, so we could not screw things up on a daily basis, like manufacturing or customer service could. So, research and development was rarely picked on. I do remember one meeting where Dave got on us for not understanding the formaldehyde chemistry in one of our amine processes, so we were not helping production solve their odor problem in a quick manner. As Dave was letting the three R&D managers in the meeting have it (and it was mostly my department with the issue), I thought, *"Dave is really giving it to us, and we do deserve it … and he is doing a really good job of tearing us a new one."* I admired his language skills and ability to slap us around. I responded to his comments, and we fixed the problem the next week.

I soon realized that the best place to sit around the huge, boardroom table was not as far from Dave as possible but right *next* to Dave. Each week, Dave would select one or two victims to question how their departments were running in an effort to get the best performance from each of us. However, it is human nature to pick someone across the table from you to attack. It is much harder to put the heat on someone right next to you. They are harder to look at, because Dave would have to turn his head a lot. Plus, no one wants to start a fight with the person next to you, as they might take it the wrong way, and it could be a more threatening situation. So, I sat next to Dave, quietly eating my sandwich, and keeping my head down, as Dave shot flamethrower comments across the table to other people. I learned a lot, and it was very entertaining.

Staying calm is much easier said than done. About 99 percent of the time, I can stay perfectly calm, even in the midst of serious insults, "Floyd, that is the dumbest thing I have seen anyone do in a long time."

My response typically might be, "You could be right." Since I don't like conflict and am not very good at it, my goal is to defuse the situation and make it go away. Hopefully, they go away and bother someone else. I do "try" to listen to the person's point of view, because they might be right, but largely, I think I took a reasonable course of action and don't respect their opinion. You can't be insulted by someone you don't respect. Ninety-nine percent of the time I can stay calm, but sometimes the 1 percent occurs, and I "z-out" (a term meaning you change personalities). Then, I say things that are best left unsaid or, in business, go over my boss's head to solve a problem. This type of activity almost always gets me in serious personal or professional trouble.

When I first got married to Pat, my father gave me some invaluable advice: "If there is something you really need to say, something you really need to tell your wife, something she's got to hear, something that really irritates you and you have to get off your chest, etc., *shut your mouth!* You won't explain it correctly, and you will make the situation worse."

Most things are not that important, and you can live with it. Telling your wife you can't stand her meatloaf or don't like spending time with her parents won't help your situation. It's best to hope she realizes her meatloaf stinks and her mother is a pain in the butt. Fortunately for me, Pat's meatloaf is excellent, and her mother was a great person. If it is more critical, like money management, it should be brought up later in a calm fashion.

Try Dave's stay calm technique in your next business meeting or family confrontation. Ideally, your calmness will defuse the situation, and everyone will get to a logical resolution. This method can also be viewed as the Christian approach to a problem. If that doesn't work, you can be entertained by watching the other person vaporize due to your calmness.

Tom—Pregnant Pause

Tom was my boss later in my career and a master of the pregnant pause. This technique is useful when trying to close a sale and dealing with a customer's purchasing manager. When dealing with one of your large customers, the salesman and his manager have to remain professional and stay calm, regardless of how ridiculous the comments and requests from the purchasing agent are. They are the customer, and you can't jeopardize current sales volume. In business, some people have no sense of fairness and will try to squeeze you for every last cent.

William, the purchasing agent, knew we had a slightly better product than our competition, and our service and delivery were also a lot better. He had worked us down to a barely profitable price, and we thought we had agreement on all the conditions, including price.

William, "Really, if our volume exceeds ten million pounds per year, I think we should get a five cent per pound rebate, and we shouldn't have to pay for freight."

Floyd's mind, *What an ass! What a cheap SOB!*

What Floyd would tend to say, "Will, I thought we had agreement on the price, and you know we can't afford to give you a rebate or pay for the delivery."

What Tom would do is *not say anything,* but just stare at William for about a minute. No matter how awkward the silence, Tom would just keep staring, hoping I could keep quiet also. Tom would just not respond to unfair or ludicrous comments. Usually, the purchasing agent will break first and say, "I guess your price is good enough, and we can move forward with this."

Try this in your next business meeting or heated family discussion. Hopefully, the silence will defuse the situation, allow rational thinking to prevail, and if nothing else, you may win the argument.

Rick—Floyd's Best Argument

I won one of my best company arguments saying very little. My division had been acquired by Witco Corporation, and various areas were being restructured or having their work changed. My research and development department in Columbus, Ohio, worked on laundry products and developed surfactants and cleaners for detergent companies. A smaller group in Toronto, Ontario, Canada, also developed cleaners and even sold some detergents to the private label market. My department was doing a good job, and we had great relationships with several key customers, like Procter & Gamble. Rick's group in Canada thought that my group should be disbanded, and his group should take over our work. Research and development management was happy with the current arrangement and did not see a need for a change. Rick kept pushing the issue and claimed my group's work was inferior and was overstepping its bounds and getting into his area of expertise. After about nine months of his constant harping, the VP of technology and the director of research demanded we have a meeting in a neutral location to iron out the problem. They chose a hotel at O'Hare Airport in Chicago. We got to the room, and Bill, the VP, asked who wanted to go first. Rick couldn't contain himself, so he wanted to go first. I agreed. Rick complained about my group for about fifteen minutes, while I sat there quietly and diligently took notes on each of his points and complaints. I didn't say a word or react to any of his comments; I only took notes. When Rick had finished ranting, they looked at me, and I started explaining my point of view and countered his complaints one at a time. Less than a minute into my rebuttal, Rick couldn't control himself and interrupted me with some more of his points. I stayed calm and waited from him to finish. Then, I started on my next point. In less than a minute, Rick interrupted me again to push his views. I stayed calm as his talked and just looked at the VP and director, hoping they could read my mind: *Can't you see what a jerk*

Rick is? Fortunately, they quickly came to the correct conclusion and stopped the discussion. "We have heard enough. Floyd's group will do the laundry research, and Rick's group will just support the business in Canada." By then, Rick realized he had hung himself with his words and rudeness, and he accepted the decision. I won easily by just being professional and hardly had to say anything. This a version of the stay calm technique, which you may want to try in your next altercation.

22. Abortion and Euthanasia

Abortion of a fetus or euthanasia of a seriously ill older patient are unbelievably difficult and emotional topics and will be the subject of a future book. I believe in both the rights of the unborn and the right of the mother to decide what happens with her body. Therein lies the conflict.

We had a friend, Ted, who was in his first semester at a community college in Cleveland. He became involved with Peggy, and they started having unprotected sex. Right or wrong, I understand why they were having sex, but the unprotected part was just foolish.

Peggy became pregnant, which resulted in much debate, arguing, and blame-setting in Ted's household. Ted's family is Catholic; some more serious than others. Later we heard that Ted's sister and his mother came to the very difficult conclusion that Peggy should have an abortion, since Peggy and Ted were in no position—financially, mentally, or emotionally—to raise a child. Ted's grandmother was the strictest Catholic in the family, attending services all the time. Surprisingly, even "Gramma" finally asked, "Why don't you just get an abortion?" Everyone almost fell over. In the end, Ted's mother took Peggy to a clinic and the pregnancy was terminated. Ted and Peggy soon broke up.

A few years later, Ted met and married Martha, and they have been married over thirty years. A few years into their marriage, they tried to have children. Martha had three miscarriages, and it became apparent that she was not going to be able to have a baby.

In retrospect, was God teaching everyone a lesson? Ted's only chance at being a father disappeared during the abortion. Was God saying, "Since you did not want your first child, you cannot have any"? Who knows, but it does not seem like a coincidence to me.

I believe God created all the animals, and animals are not inherently evil. In nature, it is common for a mother cat to kill any deformed or very weak offspring soon after birth. I assume this is to preserve her precious resource of milk. What this means, if anything, in terms of abortion is unknown, but it is food for thought.

When a male lion takes over a pride from another lion, he may kill the cubs from the previous male lion. With the cubs gone, the females go into heat within a few days. This unthinkable act is a way for the male lion to breed and gives him a good chance to produce offspring quickly.

I'm not sure how we reconcile the harshness of nature with the thinking and morality of humans. What is right? What is practical? How does our situation fit with current laws? Can we live with the decision we make? What are the alternatives? What should I do? What does God expect me to do?

23. Let There Be Light—Solar and Wind Energy

Energy and water are the keys to the future. If you look at the natural world, we have been given a lot. First, early man could find wood and start a fire. This worked for centuries but limited man's technological development. Then, oil and gas were discovered. They are easy to use by just burning, and they contain a great deal of energy per pound. Oil and gas can be transported, allowing development of moving vehicles.

Nuclear power is an interesting area. To use it, man must be quite technically sophisticated to purify and safely handle the ingredients. Nuclear power seems to be a test by God of our intellect as well as of our social responsibility to use it properly.

It seems obvious that sooner or later (ten years or two hundred years from now), we will primarily be driving electric cars charged by electricity derived from solar, wind, water, and nuclear energy sources. Carbon fuels will be reserved for airplanes, boats/ships, and possibly long-haul trucks and cars.

God seems to have given us everything we need. Look around, and we see sun, wind, and waves, all with plenty of energy to supply our needs. All these take some technology and social will to develop and use, but it looks like God has provided for us.

Are we going to use our petroleum resources effectively, or are we going to squander them and hopelessly pollute our planet? God gave us oil first, because we were not ready for solar, wind, and nuclear. But there comes a time for transition, when we should go to the pure, clean, limitless energy forms he gave us. Again, it looks like a test for mankind, and we are struggling with the decisions.

The sun provides plenty of light and heat during the day. At night, we have the moon, which is basically a night-light. Why do we need the moon? It gives us ocean tides, but do we need these? It seems someone decided we needed a night-light in case we had to go out in the dark. I find it incredible that from our viewpoint on earth, the sun and the moon appear to be the same size. During a solar eclipse, you can see they are virtually identical. The odds of this happening must be astronomical. Looks like God designed it this way.

Being a scientist, I believe in the Big Bang Theory and evolution, but I also believe God designed the end result. I do not find the scientific theories and the religious beliefs incompatible at all. Einstein believed in both, and he was a lot smarter than I am. He believed in an elegance to science and a symmetry and beauty in the physical word. Einstein spent much of his adult life striving to uncover the truth about how the universe was put together.

24. Conclusion

There is a God, and for many of us, life is good. You should try to be happy and useful. Look around, and you should see the beauty of the earth and the beauty of life. I believe God will help you if you believe in him and use your mind to solve your problems in a reasonable fashion.

If you are desperately poor, you are probably not reading this book anyway, because you have more pressing problems.

If each person tries to answer these questions, maybe he or she will lead a more purposeful and enjoyable life and result in a better world:

- What can I do to improve my life or my attitude toward life?
- What can I do to improve my family's life and interactions?
- What can I do to improve my local community and society in general?
- How can we point our politicians and leaders in the correct direction?
- How can we reduce the hate in society and between groups of people?
- How can we get where God wants us to go?

If you are in the central Ohio area, I strongly recommend the Presbyterian Church in Coshocton, Ohio, or St. Mary's Catholic Church in Delaware, Ohio. Both of these places of worship have given me comfort.

About the Author

Dr. Floyd E. Friedli grew up in Coshocton, Ohio, the son of Jean Ely Friedli and Floyd Emmett Friedli.Friedli is a longtime member of the Presbyterian Church in Coshocton. Friedli graduated from the College of Wooster in Wooster, Ohio, with a major in chemistry and a minor in music. He completed his PhD in organic chemistry at The Ohio State University in Columbus. Friedli has authored fifteen scientific papers and holds seven chemical patents. He is currently an account manager for Akzo Nobel Surface Chemistry.

Friedli has been married to Patricia Smith Friedli for thirty-four years. They have a son, Floyd Evan Friedli, an accountant. Friedli loves to play the trumpet, having studied at Wooster and Ohio State. He is a member of the Cardinal Health Orchestra, Cardinal Health Jazz Band, the Project 75 combo (project75band.com) with his wife Patricia, and the Dublin Brass Quintet (www.dublinbrass.us). Floyd and Pat compete in ballroom dancing, and his remaining spare time is taken up with travel, golf, weightlifting, and writing.

CPSIA information can be obtained at www.ICGtesting.com
Printed in the USA
BVOW032216011111

275047BV00001B/85/P